No group loves Johnny Cash more than the prisoners for whom he often performs. They know about his brushes with the law and his battle with drugs. They know that he is a survivor and a victor, one who understands, one who offers hope.

That's why Gary Mark Gilmore, during his last hours before his execution at Utah State Prison, called Johnny and asked him to sing "Amazing Grace."

Johnny Cash is only one of many Grand Ole Opry stars who can now sing with new understanding:

Amazing grace,
How sweet the sound . . . .

How Sweet the Sound

JAMES C. HEFLEY

LIVING BOOKS

Tyndale House Publishers, Inc.

Wheaton, Illinois

Scripture references are from
the King James Version of the Bible.

First printing, October 1981
Library of Congress Catalog Card Number 81-52009
ISBN 0-8423-1176-9 Living Books edition
Printed in the United States of America.

*Dedicated to
my daddy, Fred Hefley,
who loves the old songs
and
is still singing them at seventy*

CONTENTS

ACKNOWLEDGMENTS

Back in the Arkansas Ozarks I grew up listening to country music. Daddy played the guitar and sang. Many Saturday afternoons the "boys" made music around the pot-bellied stove in our country store.

At graveyard funerals I heard the comforting strains of "How Beautiful Heaven Must Be." At all-day singings and dinners on the ground I tapped my toes to "Now Let Us Have a Little Talk with Jesus" and "I'll Fly Away." At brush arbor revivals I listened to family groups harmonize on "Farther Along" and "Turn Your Radio On."

When the assignment came to write this book, I was ready emotionally and nostalgically. My Michigan, city-born wife, Marti, with whom I have collaborated on many previous books, declined to get involved, except to give loving support.

During our dating days she had once heard me say that I enjoyed "the Opry" on Saturdays. After our marriage, she learned, much to her chagrin, that I had been referring to the "Grand Ole Opry" broadcast on Saturday nights, not "grand opera" aired on Saturday afternoons. To each his own.

Before the book's completion, I made many trips to Nashville just up the Interstate from our home near Chattanooga. During those visits to Music City, I spent hours and hours backstage at the Opry, talking to performers and soaking up the atmosphere of the country music world. On Sundays I attended the churches where many country music personalities worship. Weekdays brought more interviews and long hours of research at the Country Music Foundation's Media Center.

Without the help of the capable and patient librarians at the Media Center, many stories could not have been included in this book. They have a file, it seems, on everybody who has ever recorded a country song or performed on a stage.

I have researched in libraries of many countries, including the Library of Congress, but I must say that the folks in Nashville are the most efficient and helpful of all. A thousand kudos to the Country Music Foundation for providing such a service to writers. We could not do our work without them.

More research help came from the Nashville Public Library; the Chattanooga-Hamilton Country Bicentennial Library in Chattanooga;

the University of Tennessee Main and Music Libraries; the John Edwards Foundation of Los Angeles; the Radio and Television Commission of the Southern Baptist Convention which produces the popular, syndicated radio program "Country Crossroads"; and Dr. Richard A. Peterson, a sociologist at Vanderbilt University.

At the Opry, Jerry Strobel, public relations director, was terrific. He's the type who never says something can't be done. His response to me was always "Let's see what we can do."

I cannot fail to mention the ministers in Nashville who are tuned to the spiritual needs of country music people. Especially helpful were the Reverends Jimmie Snow of Evangel Temple; Billy Ray Moore of the Lord's Chapel; Dr. Don Finto of the Belmont Church of Christ; Dr. Ralph Stone of Two Rivers Baptist Church; Joe Dee Kelley, executive director of the Assemblies of God in Tennessee; and the irreverently funny Joe Johnson, editor of inspirational books for Broadman Press at the Baptist Sunday School Board. "Hee-Haw" ought to audition Joe.

Special appreciation goes to my colleague, Ginny Waddell, a well-known free-lance writer in Nashville, who probably holds the record for the most inspirational articles written about country music personalities. A catalyst for many of the interviews in this book, Ginny provided a wealth of background information and notes.

Finally, there is the Music City Christian

Fellowship, a small but growing group of believers in the country music industry, who will undoubtedly have a great influence for God in the years ahead. What can I say but thanks to Fellowship members and to the other Christian entertainers who opened their hearts and shared what God is doing in their lives.

Despite the help I received and the long months I spent writing, the story of what God is doing among the country music fraternity must remain incomplete. This book chronicles what God has been doing only in recent years. As the Spirit keeps moving and believers keep growing, the best is yet to come.

1

I Have Returned

Nashville: Music City, U.S.A., mecca of country music, and home of the Grand Ole Opry. To this magnet come writers, singers, pickers, and fiddlers—everyone hoping to be "discovered," eager to see his or her name in lights and song at the top of the charts. They come craving to hear the words, "Ladies and gentlemen, will you welcome the star of our show. . . ."

Nashville, Spring 1959. Marijohn Wilkin, a red-headed music teacher from Sanger, Texas, just two years in Music City, has been making it as a songwriter. Right in the middle of a talent explosion, she's been working with three of country music's biggest scribes: Wayne Walker, John D. Loudermilk, and Danny Dill.

On this special evening Marijohn and John Loudermilk are brainstorming. Marijohn is at the piano, hymnbook open. She hasn't been to church in more than a month of Sundays but still loves the old familiar tunes from her Southern Baptist childhood in north Texas. Playing those hymns often helps the creative juices flow.

Loudermilk, sprawled on the floor, has scribblings all around him. At it for two hours, they still have no solid lead. Maybe the well is dry for the day.

"'When the roll is called up yonder, when the roll. . . .' John, I guess we've met our Waterloo. Shall we call it a day?"

"Waterloo . . . Waterloo," her partner croons, growing excited like a hound dog that's just picked up a hot scent. "Waterloo. . . ." Grabbing his guitar, he strikes up a chord.

Marijohn comes in on the piano and sings, "Where will you meet your Waterloo?"

"Everybody has to pay," John adds.

Then both sing, "Everybody has to meet his Waterloo."

"John, that's a hit!"

"It's the corniest thing I ever heard."

"I don't care. It's a hit. Let's write it."

A verse from Napoleon. A stanza from the Bible. A bit of rhyme. A half hour later, a million seller is on paper. Now two decades later, Stonewall Jackson still sings "Waterloo" almost every Saturday night on the Opry.

As the golden years roll by, Marijohn writes more hit songs. Performer Lefty Frizzell takes "The Long Black Veil" to the "Top Ten." Old pal Red Foley makes hay with "Travelin' Man." Webb Pierce strikes fire with "Shanghaied," written by Marijohn and Mel Tillis.

Jimmie C. Newman brings her national fame with "PT 109." John and Jacqueline Kennedy love it. Singers flock to Marijohn, seeking new material to record. Her royalties mount. Her fame as a songwriter skyrockets. Her voice is in demand, too. She works with the Jordainaires and the Anita Kerr Singers.

She makes repeated flights to New York and parties with the "beautiful people," who tell her, "You're the greatest, Marijohn, absolutely the greatest!" and "I just love that accent of yours!" and "Where ever do you get so many ideas for songs?"

The acclaim must taste sweet to the former Baylor University freshman once told she was wasting her time with voice lessons. Hardly. When the party is over and the headiness wears off, sad nostalgia rolls in. Memories of her Texas childhood wisp through her mind.

She recalls the aroma of fresh Veribest bread from the ovens in the Melson family's bakery and the sight of the Bible on her father Ernest's desk with the Texas hogleg kept in the drawer. He never used the gun, but he opened the Bible hundreds of times to the Depression bums and hoboes who found him an easy touch. Her beloved father had often plunked her on the piano stool and then, lifting his fiddle bow, had played along with her. This smiling bakery man had beamed as she belted out "Jesus Loves Me" in First Baptist Sunday school.

Her father, stricken with incurable cancer, was the most godly man she'd ever known. She'd had eleven years of straight A's when she had to start making bread deliveries for him. His pain had become so bad that he had to have morphine shots around the clock. He never complained, but she could read the suffering in his eyes. She was his only child and she hurt for him. How she wished that he could get up and play his fiddle one more time while she followed on the piano.

"Come closer, Daughter John," he whispered. "Promise me you'll go to college so you won't have to be just an ear player like me. . . . Take care of your mother. . . ." Then he was gone.

"Ernest Melson was a good man, like Bartholomew," the preacher said over his coffin. Marijohn hardly listened. The questions, the doubts, the whys were already flooding her brain. People all over Texas had been praying for her "Daddyboy" and he had died. What good was prayer, anyway?

A month later Marijohn graduated from high school with honors. Then she was off to Baylor where the music teacher told her, "Marijohn, you aren't a singer. Give up the idea."

The professor from Southwestern Baptist Theological Seminary had given her private lessons but was only a little more encouraging. "Marijohn, your voice hasn't settled. Stop singing dance band-style." Never mind that she had her own radio show. Country music wasn't approved of by her Baptist teachers.

She then transferred to Hardin-Simmons Baptist University, becoming the first and only female member of the world-famous Hardin-Simmons Cowboy Band. One night during a parade in Dallas, a handsome man on a white horse rode up beside her and announced, "Howdy, I'm Tex Ritter."

Tex got her an audition for the movies. The producer offered her a contract for a western film. Marijohn thanked him kindly, but said, "I promised my daddy I would finish school." There was another reason: handsome Bedford Russell, her football player sweetheart.

She and Bedford married right after graduation during World War II. He went into the Army Air Force. She lived on base during his flight training and found herself caught up in a world far different from her sheltered childhood. It was a dizzy, exciting whirl of newly-wed joy and drinking and dancing at the officers' club.

Her dashing pilot got his wings and orders for North Africa. A year later came the telegram, "We regret to inform you. . . ." Captain Russell had been taken prisoner and been put on an Italian sub. British planes caught the sub in the middle of the Mediterranean. His body could not be recovered.

Twenty-one and widowed, Marijohn took a job teaching music, began drinking more, and remarried too soon. Then at twenty-nine, divorced, and a mother, she moved to Springfield, Missouri. Her young son, Bucky, got a job for twenty-five dollars a week singing on Red Foley's "Country Jamboree." Marijohn couldn't find employment.

In the early fifties, Red Foley was "Mr. Country Music," the first country artist to sell a million records. Red could warm up the coldest audience when he went offstage into the audience and sang "Shake a Hand." He could turn a nightclub into a church with "Steal Away." His trademark song, "Peace in the Valley," the first gospel song to sell a million records, could quiet the noisiest fans.

Red had attended Georgetown, a Southern Baptist college in Kentucky. He also had a trail of tragedy and heartache behind him. His first wife, Pauline, had died giving birth to their daughter Betty. His second wife, Eva, had given him their daughter Shirley. Eva reportedly died of a broken heart after Red began seeing a nightclub singer.

When Eva died, Red married the singer. His teenaged daughter, Shirley, eloped with a young Nashville preacher named Pat Boone.

One night in Marijohn's home, Red took a can opener and carved his signature in her kitchen table. But who could be angry at Red, a shower of sunshine with a good word for everybody, a man who could make everyone happy but himself? When he sang "Peace in the Valley," tears glistened in his eyes, yet Red, who could comfort others, had no peace himself.

Haunted by guilt over his second wife's death, he tried to drown his misery in alcohol. He could hold his liquor, and few fans knew his troubles. But Marijohn and other friends knew that the great country artist was drinking himself to death.

Marijohn finally started singing in a piano bar to supplement Bucky's earnings. She felt guilty about promoting drinking, when alcohol was destroying Red Foley, Hank Williams, and other great talents. But she kept telling herself, "Things will get better. It can't be much worse." She sought no solace in the God of her childhood. She would go it alone.

One night a lawyer heard her in the bar. "Hey, you're pretty good," he said. "You ought to be in Nashville. If you're going to shoot tigers, go where the tigers are."

With less than $100 she packed up little Bucky and headed for Tennessee. Like other hopeful musicians swarming to Music City, she took whatever job she could get while waiting for the big break.

One evening she was singing in a Nashville piano bar called "The Voodoo." An advertising executive stayed for hours, downing drink after drink and listening to her sing. Finally he wobbled out the door, climbed into his car, and almost killed himself in a wreck. When Marijohn heard that he was critically injured, she felt terrible. "God help me break out of this," she moaned. It was not so much a prayer as a cry of desperation. A week later she was working as a songwriter at Cedarwood Publishing for Jim Denny, one of the biggest names in country music. She was on her way up and God was only a memory.

Her big hits came rapidly: "Make the Water-wheel Roll" with Mel Tillis; "Dying for Love," recorded by Jimmie C. Newman; and "Good-night, Mama, Goodnight, Papa" by old friend Red Foley, who had moved to Nashville. Then her sponsor, Jim Denny, died from cancer.

It all seemed so unfair. First her father, then Bedford, and now the kindly publisher who had given her a chance in songwriting. She was angry at God but wouldn't admit it. She'd show him and the world. She got a partner and opened her own house, Buckhorn Publishing, named for Bucky.

Buckhorn came at a propitious time: Country music was booming in Nashville. The Grand Ole Opry was drawing thousands of fans every weekend to hear Roy Acuff, Red Foley, Patsy Cline, Kitty Wells, the sensational new Loretta Lynn, Cowboy Copas, Billy Walker, and other stars. The performers and the songwriters who kept them supplied with hits were like family to Marijohn. When one suffered, they all did.

Early in March 1963 three of the biggest stars in town were returning by private plane from a show in Kansas City. Just short of Nashville their plane crashed in a heavy thunderstorm. Searchers found their torn bodies in the wreckage. Then another star was killed in an auto crash on the way to the funeral.

Besides Jim Denny's death from cancer and the sudden loss of four more good friends in accidents, her son, Bucky, was making it in country music and didn't need his mother's tutelage anymore. Marijohn felt grief-stricken and alone.

The rhymes and the music wouldn't come. She started hating songwriting. Tired of fighting and yielding to depression, she became a recluse in a little house in the country.

Thanksgiving Day, 1964. Marijohn took all the pills and aspirin she could find in the house and lay down to die. Red Foley and Mel Tillis showed up to spoil her plan.

"Marijohn, how many pills did you take?" Red shouted.

"D-d-don't you e-e-e-ver d-do this a-gain," stuttered Mel.

Mel and Red snapped her out of the depression. She traveled to the Far East with a USO troupe. Then, back home after New Year's, she felt the melancholy return.

She'd read about someone committing suicide with a rifle. On Easter morning, about 5:00 A.M., she took her gun, placed the butt on the floor, laid the end of the barrel along her neck, and squeezed the trigger. The bullet zinged past her ear, ricocheted off the wall, and bounced harmlessly back on the floor. She tried again. Pushing the gun barrel closer to her temple, she squeezed the trigger. Again the bullet deflected.

Fingering a misshapen piece of lead, she sat on the floor in a daze. "I can't even kill myself," she mumbled. Then she was struck by a thought—the God she had left behind must be trying to tell her something. As her eyes moistened, she let the tears come. For the first time in years she cried. When fingers of dawn began filtering through the windows, she stopped.

Bundling up her courage, she returned to work.

A tape with a letter arrived from an American soldier in Germany. "I'm a fellow Texan," he wrote. "Your cousin said I should send this to you. I'll look you up when I come to Nashville." It was signed "Captain Kris Kristofferson." She had never heard of him.

Marijohn had always been an easy mark for aspiring young musicians. This one was different from most. He had class and polish; he had also been a Rhodes Scholar and a helicopter pilot. He had even written short stories which were published in the *Atlantic Monthly* and had been invited to teach at West Point. "I'm gonna make us both rich," he promised Marijohn.

She had heard that before, but she felt Kris was an unusual talent. She signed the clean-cut, scholarly youth to a Buckhorn contract and gave him a small advance to supplement the minimal wage he was getting as a janitor at nearby Columbia Records.

Kristofferson and the other young artists who looked up to Marijohn and members of the Nashville establishment were restless in their search for meaning in life. Marijohn couldn't help them there, for she was still searching herself. Lately into Buddhism and fortune-telling, she was holding seances at her house.

Living by impulse, she thought a long, leisurely trip to Europe might help. En route to Rome, she felt the urge to take a ship across the Mediterranean. She had the uncanny sense that she would know when the ship passed the spot where Bedford had been killed over twenty years before.

The luxury liner *Michelangelo* was on the sea a night and a day when it began pitching and rocking. The second evening Marijohn sat in the dining room, telling a new friend about Bedford and trying to hold the dishes on the shaky table.

"I'm sure I'll know the place when we reach it," she said. At eleven o'clock she began crying uncontrollably. She looked at her friend and sobbed, "This is it. This is where Bedford went down. I'm sure this is the spot."

She asked him to join her in a walk on the deck. As they emerged into the salty air, the wind suddenly stopped blowing. Standing before a sea which had become smooth as glass, she felt a sudden release. It was as if a tremendous load had been lifted. The hurt from Bedford's death, over which she had never been able to cry before, was gone.

She spent a few days singing in Rome, enjoyed a week of rest with actor-singer Dennis Weaver and his wife, Jerry, and then journeyed to Israel to see the holy places familiar from Baptist Sunday school and Training Union days. Drawn along by an invisible Force, she felt herself on a pilgrimage, bound for she knew not where.

Back in Nashville both good and bad news greeted her. Kris Kristofferson's "For the Good Times," a Buckhorn property, was a gigantic hit. Kris was making it. The bad news was that her partner in Buckhorn had terminal cancer.

Then her mother passed away. Next her eighty-three-year-old uncle became gravely ill. As the closest relative, Marijohn felt duty-bound to care for him. Her publishing company floundered under poor management while she was away, and she returned to face possible financial ruin.

She dismissed the thought of seeing a preach-er for counsel. The ones she remembered pointed their fingers and preached hell-fire and dam-nation. She could see herself telling a pastor her story and hearing the stern voice say, "You made your bed. Now repent or lie in it." She couldn't take that.

Flipping through the Yellow Pages, she saw "Dial-a-Prayer" and a telephone number. She dialed. "God loves you. He cares," the recorded voice assured.

There was another number for those who wanted personal counsel from the "Dial-a-Prayer" minister. She called for an appoint-ment.

When Marijohn emerged from her shiny, midnight blue Cadillac, the young minister saw an attractive red-haired woman in lizard-skin boots and a full-length mink coat worn over a tailored shirt and jeans.

"How may I help you?" he asked.

"I guess I have every problem anybody can have, young man."

"You look healthy." Then glancing through the window at her Cadillac, he said, "And prosperous. What are your problems?"

She briefly told him of the mess she was in.

"Well, why don't we just thank God for all this?" he said.

Marijohn stared at him in surprise. "I guess I never thought of that, but I'll try."

The preacher prayed. Then she got into her car and drove back to her farmhouse outside Nashville. She cried all the way, praying over and over, "Thank you, Lord. I don't know why, but thank you. Thank you."

She never again saw the young preacher who helped her open the door to restored fellowship with the Savior of her childhood.

As she read her Bible and prayed constantly during the next few days, one line kept running through her mind, "I have returned . . . I have returned."

She knew a song was coming on and wrote:

I have returned to the God of my childhood,
To the same simple faith as a child I knew.

The words rushed like a torrent:

Like the prodigal son, I longed for my loved ones,
For the comforts of home and the God I outgrew.

And another verse:

I have returned to the Yahweh of Judah

On my knees I did fall where the wall now stands.

This lesson I learned as I've worked my way homeward:

The Savior of all is a comfort to man.*

The reality of problems which hadn't gone away loomed before her. "How can I make it, Lord?" The answer came, *Let me help you, one day at a time.* That was the secret, and she started to put it in a song.

After muddling through a few lines, she asked Kris Kristofferson to help. Working together, they completed in little time what would become the most popular gospel song in history, "One Day at a Time."

Since then, Marijohn Wilkin has written hundreds of gospel songs. Some are sung every Saturday night on the Grand Ole Opry, on national television shows, and by performers in many languages around the world. She herself has sung on television where she has frequently told how God brought her back to the faith of her childhood.

"It took a long time for God to deal with me," she says. "I had to go through a lot of deep water, but thank God, I've finally found what life is all about."

The story of Marijohn, who still has her offices on Nashville's Music Row, parallels what has happened to many more country music artists. The first line of her song, "I

*From the song by Marijohn Wilkin, "I Have Returned."

have returned to the God of my childhood," is the testimony of many of her colleagues. When their lives fell apart, they, like Marijohn, returned to the God of their childhood.

Of course, not every Christian entertainer in Nashville has experienced the ravages of success. Some have managed to stay off the prodigal trail. But many in recent years have been like the prodigal of Luke 15, who lived high, lost it all, and fell into the pig sty before he came to his senses and declared, "I will arise and go to my father. . . . "

Their names are familiar to every lover of country music: Johnny Cash, Teddy Wilburn, Billy Walker, Donna Stoneman, Connie Smith, Skeeter Davis, Vic Willis, Jimmie Snow, Bobby Wood, Billy Grammer, and many more.

This book is about them and other country music celebrities who love the Lord and mean every word of the hymns and gospel songs they sing in public. The stories are about spiritual rebirth or the rekindling of faith—about God working to bring the warm wind of spiritual revival into Nashville's present-day music scene.

2

*Roots and
Religion*

"Most of us grew up around country churches
and small-town congregations," says Bill Anderson, member of the Grand Ole Opry since
1962 and star of his own syndicated country
music television show. "I don't believe there
are a half-dozen persons of the Opry who didn't
start out by singing in a church choir, singing
religious songs, or maybe singing in a family
unit that traveled as a religious group."

Anderson, like Marijohn Wilkin and Kris
Kristofferson, doesn't fit the stereotype of the
ignorant hillbilly. A former deejay and graduate in journalism from the University of
Georgia, he acknowledges the influence of
his grandfather, a Methodist preacher.

Roy Acuff, now seventy-seven, is an institution in country music. His father, also a
preacher, made an impact on his life at an
early age. "I was raised by the Bible in a

Christian family," says the "King of Country Music," a title given to him by his friend Dizzy Dean. "I went to the Baptist Young People's Union and Sunday school, hardly missing a Sunday before coming to Nashville and going on the road as a musician."

Reverend Neil Acuff, Roy's father, once pastored the Fountain City Baptist Church near Knoxville, Tennessee, practiced law, and also served as an elected judge. When Roy began carousing during his teenaged years, his father pointed out the consequences of his waywardness. "You're going to be a leader," he predicted. "You've got to live up to that responsibility."

Now thousands journey to Nashville just to hear Roy sing "The Wabash Cannonball" and "The Great Speckled Bird" and to watch him yo-yo and balance his fiddle bow on his nose. Hanging on the door of dressing room number one backstage at the new Opry House is the plaque which sums up his attitude: "There ain't nuthin' gonna come up today that me and the Lord can't handle."

If Roy Acuff is the king of country music, then Johnny Cash is the swashbuckling crown prince. His dramatic turnaround from drinking, womanizing, and pill-popping is well known. However, few have heard of his boyhood back in the Arkansas delta where his family never missed church on Sundays and Wednesday nights.

A solid streak of piety runs through the Cash ancestry. Since the seventeenth century, every family will has opened with "In the name of

God, Amen ..." and has closed with "hope and faith in the resurrection of our Lord. . . ." Johnny's paternal grandfather was a Baptist preacher; his maternal grandfather led singing in a Methodist church for forty years. Johnny's father, Ray, is a deacon and Sunday school teacher.

Years later when Johnny hit rock bottom and many predicted he was a goner, he turned back to the God of his childhood. "I found myself through the faith I knew as a child," he would say.

Sonny James began as Little James Loden of Hackleburg, Alabama's singing Loden family. They sang in church services and at singing conventions.

Wilma Lee Cooper, wife of the late Stoney Cooper, developed a repertoire of gospel songs from singing with her family, the Learies, beside the pump organ at home. They provided inspiration in churches, comfort at funerals, and entertainment at community social events.

Willie Nelson, Jimmy Carter's favorite country entertainer, grew up in a Methodist church in Texas and sang in the choir. "I learned to love gospel songs and still do," Willie says. After his parents divorced, Willie's mother left him and his sister, Bobbi, with their devout grandmother because she wanted him to have a Christian upbringing. Willie's grandmother penned gospel songs and Willie himself began writing them at an early age.

At age six Larry Gatlin began singing gospel songs in Texas with his two younger brothers,

Steve and Rudy. Their mother was the pianist; they were later joined by their younger sister, LaDonna. Larry says, "God meant for me to write and sing with my family, not just to entertain, but to move and touch people."

The one and only Dolly Parton was brought up in the Church of God in Sevierville, Tennessee. "It was a very free church," she says. "If anybody wanted to get up and sing or shout his feelings, he could do it." Her grandfather, the Reverend Jake Owens (still the pastor), was the model for her song, "Old-time Preacher Man." Dolly says that when she's home in Sevierville "and they're having a revival, I go and sing as I used to do when I was a girl back there."

As a boy, Hank Williams sat on the piano bench beside his mother, while she played the piano for services at their church in Alabama.

Roy Drusky, who has had over fifty records on the charts and ten number ones, sang in the youth choir at Moreland Baptist Church in Georgia. His mother was church pianist.

Blind Ronnie Millsap, born in the hills around Robinsville, North Carolina, also "sang in church and enjoyed the gospel songs that were so much a part of my heritage."

Hank Snow gave his first performance in a church hall.

Conway Twitty not only sang in churches, but also preached for two-and-a-half years during his teens. When he heard that some church leaders were cheating people, he became disillusioned and quit the pulpit. But not music.

Gene Autry sang his first solo in the Indian Creek Baptist Church in Tioga, Texas. His grandfather, the Reverend William Autry, was the pastor.

Jeannie C. Riley, of "Harper Valley P.T.A." fame, cherishes "precious memories" of a grandfather who preached for fifty years. She too sang at church and at school functions.

Bobby Woods, who once worked with Elvis Presley and is one of the top studio musicians in Nashville, says his family was "singing before I was born." The Woods Family "sang at churches and all over, whether we got a donation or not. My grandfather was a music teacher who went around to the churches, teaching Stamps Baxter quartet songs."

Bobbie Gentry, best known for her "Ode to Billy Joe," was raised on a farm with her grandparents in Chicksaw County, Mississippi. She wrote her first song before she was seven years old. "The church was terribly important to us and it was there that I learned my music," she remembers. "I taught myself to play by watching Ginny Sue, the pianist at the Pleasant Grove Baptist Church."

Connie Smith, who has sung at the Presidential Prayer Breakfast, was reared in church.

George Hamilton IV, perhaps the biggest country music star in Europe, also grew up in church.

Jeannie Pruett says she sings "The Old

Rugged Cross" just as she did back home in Alabama.

George Jones' mother was a church pianist.

The Wilburn Family, now the Wilburn Brothers, started by singing in churches and schoolhouses in the Arkansas and Missouri Ozarks.

Tom T. Hall, the "Storyteller of Country Music," is one of eight children from a Kentucky Appalachian family. His father was a minister in Olive Hill, Kentucky.

The popular Hagar Brothers' duo on "Hee-Haw" came from a preacher's home in Illinois.

Rita Coolidge is a preacher's daughter.

The list could go on. But there are more than the personal connections between the performers and religious music.

Country music itself, especially the traditional songs, was largely cradled in the fundamentalist Christianity of rural and small-town Southern Appalachia. By the estimate of country music's greatest living historian, Dr. Bill Malone, there was "no greater influence on country music than Southern religious life, both as to the nature of the songs and to the manner in which they were performed."

Early music varied from gospel songs, such as "Will the Circle Be Unbroken?" to ballads of tragedy like "The Sinking of the Titanic"; from earthy ditties such as "Who Bit the Wart off Grandma's Nose?" with their comic relief to the fast rhythm of fiddle classics like "Turkey in the Straw." The songs reflected the beliefs of the people: Life is hard, but sometimes funny; love is sweet and parting bitter; death is certain and often tragic; and God and heaven are real.

Southern folk music remained isolated in the southern mountains until the twenties when a few musicians began venturing out to radio stations and to recording sessions advertised in circulars and county newspapers. In 1922 WSB, Atlanta, was the first station to feature country music. One of the most popular writer-performers on WSB was the Reverend Andrew Jenkins, a blind gospel singer. Within five years, fiddles were sawing, guitars twanging, and nasal voices vocalizing on WBAP, Fort Worth; on WLS, Chicago; and on WSM, Nashville.

The phonograph, or gramophone, predated radio, but few country music records were made before 1924. That year, Ernest "Pop" Stoneman was working in a mill in Bluefield, West Virginia, when he heard Henry Whittier singing on a record. Pop wrote Columbia and Okeh Records in New York: "Give me a chance and I'll do better."

Both companies offered auditions if Pop would come to New York. He saved his wages all summer and made the trip. During the next four years, Ernest and Hattie Stoneman recorded over 200 songs. Their biggest record, "The Sinking of the Titanic," sold over a million, but they earned only a few hundred dollars from it.

Though probably not the most influential, the Stonemans have to be reckoned among the founders of modern country music. Pop was born in 1893 and reared in a lob cabin in the Blue Ridge Mountains of Virginia. After meeting Hattie Frost at a Quaker church, he courted her for seven years, walking an estimated 5,200 miles between his house and hers. Hattie gave birth to twenty-three children (including five sets of twins) out of which fifteen survived.

"My folks weren't Catholics, just passionate Baptists," daughter Ronnie, now a comic on "Hee-Haw," jokes. As each child got old enough to hold an instrument, Pop would tune an instrument he had made, leave it on a bed, and warn the child, "Don't you touch this while I'm gone." Soon there were enough Stonemans for three hillbilly bands.

It was hard enough for a bachelor country musician to keep body and soul together in the thirties and early forties, much less a family the size of the Stonemans. But Pop took other jobs, usually carpentry, only when absolutely necessary. Music was the love of his life and he was determined not to quit.

Eddie Stoneman remembers cutting grass for neighbors just so he could use their bathtub when the Stonemans lived in an old Virginia farmhouse outside Washington, D.C. After moving to Maryland, Pop built a one-room shack with a canvas roof. At times the children had to solicit food at fire and police stations. Once, daughter Patsy fainted from hunger in school.

Pop and Eddie played and sang for Arthur Godfrey's radio show in 1935. That brought in a few jobs paying from a dollar fifty to ten dollars a show. They sang religious songs on a radio station and got stacks of fan mail. But the station owner couldn't pay them a living wage and the group went off the air.

Pop would go anywhere to get the family onstage. "We were always in trouble with school boards," son Dean recalls.

Finally, after World War II they were invited to perform in Washington's Constitution Hall. The show was telecast, but the children were unaware of the cameras. Donna came home from school and told Ronnie a girl from school had seen them on television. "What's television?" Ronnie asked.

Their fortune turned in the fifties. Pop won $20,000 on a television quiz show. Scott won the annual National Fiddling Championship seven times. Part of the family took first place on Arthur Godfrey's "Talent Show."

They moved to Nashville to sing on the Grand Ole Opry and in the sixties secured sponsors for their own nationally syndicated television show, "Those Stonemans." In 1967 the Country Music Association voted them "Vocal Group of the Year." Then in 1979 nine Stoneman children performed at the Museum of Natural History in Washington in recognition of the pioneer role their family had played in country music.

Ernest Stoneman died in 1968 at seventy-five; Hattie passed away in 1976. The children still hold a family reunion every August on Sand Mountain, Alabama, where hundreds of fans come to hear them sing the old hymns and ballads and do the comedy routines developed by their father.

More influential than the Stonemans was the legendary Carter Family: Doc, Sara, and Maybelle, all devout Christians.

From Stoneman country to Carter country in Virginia is less than seventy-five miles southwest as the crow flies. One of nine children, Doc (Alvin Pleasant) Carter was born in 1891 in a log cabin near the Maces Spring community, just a few miles from the Cumberland Gap. A tall, lean, jug-eared, long-nosed hillbilly, Doc played the guitar and fiddle and sold fruit trees around the area.

One selling trip took him over the mountain to the Copper Creek settlement. Always on the lookout for other musicians, Doc met a dark-haired, black-eyed mountain girl named Sara Doughtery. She played the autoharp, banjo, and guitar, and sang the old ballads and hymns with a voice as clear as a cow bell on a frosty morning. He was twenty-four and she was fifteen when they married.

The third member of the musical family came along eleven years later when Sara's comely cousin Maybelle married Doc's brother Ezra J. (Eck). The three formed a trio with Sara singing lead, Maybelle alto, and Doc bass. Ezra farmed and provided them with produce.

Doc had already been leading the choir at the Friendly Grove Methodist Church. He and the two cousins sang there, as well as at other churches and for various social affairs in the area. Doc thought they were pretty good and got excited when he learned that Ralph Peer of the Victor Talking Machine Company was coming to nearby Bristol to record country musicians.

The announcement Doc saw noted that the Stoneman Family was coming and would be recording for $100 a day. It sounded almost too good to be true.

Doc and Sara now had two children, and his parents felt it was time for him to settle down and sell fruit trees, or at least farm. Maybelle was in her seventh month of pregnancy with her first child, and Ezra didn't want her to travel the twenty-five miles to Bristol over rough roads. But Doc was determined and offered to clear a patch of weeds for Ezra if he'd let Maybelle make the trip. Ezra finally gave in and they loaded their instruments into Doc's Model A and started for Bristol.

The Stonemans had already departed when the Carters arrived in late July 1927. Doc, Sara, and Maybelle got in line with scores of other musicians who had come by bus, horse and buggy, car, train, and on foot. They waited their turn to record in the rug-draped studio on the second floor of an old warehouse. When Ralph Peer a shrewd judge of talent, heard their clear, natural voices, he immediately recognized their talent. He recorded "Bury Me under the Weeping Willow," "Wandering

Boy," "Poor Orphan Child," and three other Carter Family songs on three records. Sara sang lead and played the guitar. Maybelle sang alto and accompanied on the autoharp. Doc sang his usual bass.

Peer gave them the astounding amount of $300 in advance money on record royalties (about one-half cent per record sold) for the six songs. He and Doc also agreed that the songs would be copyrighted under the name "A. P. Carter" for publication by Peer's Southern Music Publishing Company.

The Carters left in triumph. Two days later a skinny, sickly yodeler named Jimmie Rodgers showed up. A railroad brakeman from Meridian, Mississippi, he had been singing on the radio in Asheville, North Carolina, and had seen the announcement.

The "Singing Brakeman," also called the "Blue Yodeler," was much the opposite of the moral, deeply religious, family-oriented Carters. His mother had died when he was six, and he had been bandied among relatives until, at age thirteen, he ran away with a medicine show. When this job petered out, he worked on the railroad and learned blues songs, as well as guitar and banjo-playing, from black section-hands.

He married Stella McWilliams but couldn't support her and their daughter Kathryn. His wife finally took the child home to the McWilliams grandparents.

Without waiting for a divorce, he began courting Carrie Williamson, the sixteen-year-old daughter of a Methodist preacher and promised her he would go to church. He did go at least once. As soon as he could get free of Stella, they eloped and broke her family's heart. Carrie couldn't reform him either. He spent money as fast as he made it on women and liquor. "I want to live," he'd say. "You wait, Carrie, someday I'll amount to something."

Carrie must have known that he had a girl in every town where he made music or traveled with the railroad. Still, she stayed with him and bore him a daughter, Anita, in 1921. A second daughter, June, was born two years later and died soon after birth. Jimmie was away and had to pawn his banjo to get back for the infant's funeral.

When "The Blue Yodeler" came to Bristol, he already knew he had tuberculosis and probably just a few years to live. He coughed and wheezed and had difficulty recording. Peer got only two songs, "The Soldier's Sweetheart" and a lullaby, "Sleep, Baby, Sleep."

Five weeks later Jimmie Rodgers went to New York and registered at an expensive hotel, telling the clerk that the Victor Company would pay the bill. He then brashly called Ralph Peer to say that he was in town for more recordings.

Half a year later the sickly railroad man was earning $2,000 per month. Most of his songs were being written by his first wife's sister, Elsie McWilliams. Her only previous writing experience had been preparing devotional studies for her church.

Meanwhile, Doc Carter was scouring the mountains of Virginia for songs. Coaxing his Model A over rough roads and often having to walk to more remote settlements, he said to everyone he met, "Tell me the old songs your family loves best."

Doc didn't worry with records of authorship and made any changes that he thought would improve a song. He never realized that, more than anyone else, he was building a repository of music that would preserve traditional ballads and provide a foundation for a multi-million dollar industry.

Between song-hunting excursions, Doc, Sara, and Maybelle performed in towns around the region. Since they were professionals now, Doc advertised their shows with handbills.

LOOK!
VICTOR ARTIST A. P. CARTER
AND THE CARTER FAMILY
WILL GIVE A MUSICAL PROGRAM AT _____
ON _____
COME ONE AND ALL
ADMISSION 15¢ & 25¢
GUARANTEED MORALLY GOOD

The Carters stayed close to home, while Jimmie Rodgers performed in large cities. His record sales soared. His income climbed to $100,000 a year, a stupendous sum during the early part of the Great Depression. Younger and more healthy singers were already imitating both his yodeling and his lonesome style.

Carter records were also selling well. Their hymns and mountain ballads and Jimmie Rodgers' songs could be heard on Victrolas from Maine to California. They were as well known as President Herbert Hoover among rural people.

In 1931 Ralph Peer brought Jimmie and the Carter Family together for recording sessions in Louisville. In intense pain, Jimmie left a trail of blood from frequent coughing spasms and could not stay onstage for more than twenty minutes at a time. He was making more than the President of the United States, yet he refused to slow down. Doctors warned him that he was shortening his life with cigarettes and alcohol, but he refused to give up either.

In Louisville Jimmie cut "The Wonderful City," the only hymn he ever recorded, written by his former sister-in-law Elsie McWilliams. He was so weak that Maybelle Carter had to play his guitar while he sang.

The Singing Brakeman was now on his last downgrade. Hat still cocked jauntily on his head, he looked like a walking dead man when he sauntered onstage. When he recorded, he often had to rest on a cot between recordings. His teenaged daughter, Kathryn, by his first wife, was suing him for child support.

Stories were spreading that his very patient second wife, Carrie, was about to leave him for good.

In May 1933 he went to New York to cut more records. A matronly nurse was looking after him in a hotel. On the evening of the twenty-fifth, she stopped outside his room. Hearing him cough, she checked and found him hemorrhaging blood. Since he'd already been bleeding frequently, she waited until the bleeding stopped and then went on to her room.

Just before midnight, she returned to find him hemorrhaging again. Alarmed, the nurse was unable to locate the hotel doctor immediately. Before they could get him to a hospital, the Blue Yodeler slipped into a coma and drowned in his own blood. The "father" of modern honky-tonk music and the first person to later be installed in the Country Music Hall of Fame was dead at thirty-five.

Jimmie Rodgers' body was put on a special car and taken by train to Meridian. Hundreds gathered around the railroad station where he had hung out as a boy. Late in the night they heard the low, funereal moan of an engine's whistle, the sound which Jimmie Rodgers had learned to mimic so well. Then the train pulled into the station and the hometown folk surged forward to catch a glimpse of his coffin. He had shown them—he'd become a star.

He was buried in a country cemetery beside his baby daughter, June. Hearing of his death, his first wife, Stella, sat through the night, playing his records over and over. Seven years later his oldest daughter, Kathryn, the one who had sued him for child support, swallowed a fatal dose of disinfectant.

Doc and Sara Carter were now having marital problems. Doc had kept up with the career of Jimmie Rodgers and wanted to launch out into the big cities. Sara wanted to spend more time at home with their family. They had two daughters and were expecting a third child. When Doc would not give up his musical ambitions, Sara took the children and went back to her relatives. Three years later she got a divorce, then a rare and shocking thing in southwest Virginia.

Amazingly during that same year, 1936, the Carters signed a contract with the controversial "Dr." John R. Brinkley to sing on the powerful border station, XER, which he had paid the Mexican government to build across from Del Rio, Texas. Sara took the children to Texas but refused to be reconciled with Doc. Maybelle's husband, Ezra, went down as soon as he could leave his railroad job.

Brinkley paid them only seventy-five dollars a week but gave them six months vacation a year. With the Carter Family singing mountain hymns and ballads, he made millions from hawking patent medicines to unsophisticated listeners. The cream for the Carters came in increased record sales as millions tuned in every night, except Sunday, to catch their program, which began with the song, "Keep on the Sunny Side of Life."

Doc still managed the group. As religious as ever, he was now giving 70 percent of his money to Christian causes. Stoical and moody, he kept his personal feelings to himself. Any hopes he had of winning Sara back were dashed when she married his cousin, Coy Bayes, on a trip home in 1939. The wedding took place in the home church, Mount Vernon Methodist. Ezra Carter was best man and Maybelle maid-of-honor. Doc watched sadly from the back of the church.

The clan returned to Texas the next day for one more season. Maybelle and Ezra's daughters, June, Helen, and Anita, began performing.

In 1940 they moved to WBT, Charlotte, North Carolina. Three years later the original Carter Family disbanded; Sara and her second husband, Coy Bayes, moved to California. Maybelle and her three daughters performed in Richmond, Virginia, for some time and then joined Red Foley's "Ozark Jamboree" in Springfield, Missouri.

On the way, they stopped in Nashville where they picked up a starving, young guitar player named Chet Atkins. They took him on to Missouri for his send-off to fame. Ezra Carter was also with them—he'd quit his railroad job to manage the career of his wife and daughters. Doc, who had started the original Carter Family, remained in Maces Spring, ran a general store, and filled his lonely hours with church work.

"Mother Maybelle and the Carter Sisters," as they were billed, toured for a few months with the young Assembly-of-God country singer named Elvis Presley. In 1950 Maybelle, Ezra, and their girls moved on to Nashville and the Grand Ole Opry, while Elvis rocked to stardom with the new rock-and-roll craze.

Mother Maybelle and her daughters remained with the Opry for seventeen years. When the children went their separate ways, she toured the folk festivals, appearing with Woody Guthrie and Bob Dylan. June Carter became an actress and appeared on "Jim Bowie" and "Gunsmoke." June's marriage with musician Carl Smith failed, and she started working again with her mother and sisters.

The newly reunited "Mother Maybelle and the Carter Sisters" toured with Johnny Cash, whom they had met while working with Elvis. Johnny's marriage was on the rocks and he was battling with drugs. Maybelle and Ezra, who still had a strong marriage, tried to help him. June was concerned too, for she was in love with the husky, deep-throated singer from Arkansas.

Doc died a lonely and disappointed man in 1969. He was buried in the graveyard of the Mount Vernon Methodist Church. A gold record, sculpted on his rose marble stone, was marked with the simple inscription:

A. P. CARTER
KEEP ON THE SUNNY SIDE

Sara Carter Bayes died in 1971. Johnny Cash sang one of her favorite hymns, "Farther On," at her funeral. She was buried in the church cemetery, just down the hill from Doc's plot. Ezra Carter died in 1975.

Mother Maybelle followed in 1978 and was given one of the biggest funerals in Nashville history. The service began with a slow piano verson of "The Wabash Cannonball." Tom T. Hall sang "Keep on the Sunny Side," while the congregation sang along and clapped hands. Chet Atkins strummed Maybelle's most famous guitar number, "Wildwood Flower," and Jan Howard sang "No One Stands Alone."

Johnny Cash, in his trademark black suit and white, ruffled shirt, delivered a short eulogy and read tributes from President Jimmy Carter, Evangelist Billy Graham, and other luminaries. In a voice choked with emotion Johnny said, looking down at the bronze coffin, "Here we have the empty shell of Maybelle Carter. But her soul lives forever.

"She was my friend, fellow-worker, mother-in-law, and fishing buddy. And she was a good Christian. I never heard Mother speak an unkind word in the eighteen years that I knew her."

Then friends and relatives, filing by her open coffin, sang "Will the Circle Be Unbroken?"

Mother Maybelle's death ended an era in country music. Said E. W. "Bud" Wendell, general manager of the Opry: "The influence of the Carters is so great it can't be measured. Every country music performer owes something to this family."

One of the finest tributes was penned by Gene Thorpe of the *Atlanta Journal*:

> The Carters' music compares with today's country music as a virgin compares to a prostitute. . . . The Carters sang of life's verities; today's singers sing of some girl trembling as she drops her gown to the floor. . . . The Carters' songs are timeless.

The Carters, the Stonemans, and to some extent, the songs of Jimmie Rodgers had their deepest roots in the Bible-belt culture of the rural South. And so have many in the generation which followed them.

But roots are not enough. As Teddy Wilburn, who was spiritually reborn in 1976, puts it: "A lot of performers have cut their teeth on Christian music and were raised in churches. But that doesn't mean they're Christians. Singing about God and the Bible and knowing the clichés of religion are not enough. You've got to have a personal relationship with God."

3
Nashville's Bad Boy Gets a New Manager

On a cold and foggy February night in 1937, a boy was born in Halifax, Nova Scotia's Salvation Army Hospital. He was destined to become "pastor to the stars" of country music a quarter century later. Like the United States, Canada was then mired in the Great Depression. The boy's father, Clarence E. "Hank" Snow, peddled fish and gave guitar lessons to support his family. He couldn't afford a regular hospital or even a baby bed when mother and son came home. The infant slept in a bureau drawer.

When the boy was two, Hank plopped him on a stack of Coca Cola cases at a music show and announced, "Ladies and gentlemen, may I present my son, Jimmie Rodgers Snow, named after my idol in country music." With Hank accompanying on the guitar, little Jimmie belted out, "Jesus Loves Me," a song he had learned at the Anglican church on the hill overlooking Halifax Harbor.

Billing himself "The Singing Ranger," Hank was one of a dozen rising young country singers—including Gene Autry, Bob Wills, Eddie Arnold, Red Foley, Hank Williams, and T. Tex Tyler—who were building their style around the lonesome railroad songs of the tubercular brakeman. Since he was so far away in remote eastern Canada, Hank had a tougher time becoming successful, but he was determined. By Jimmie's first birthday, Hank had a recording contract with Victor and was making show tours across the eastern provinces.

As soon as Jimmie was old enough to travel, he went on the road with his parents. Father and son performed. Mother Minnie handled the bookings and box office and then went ahead to rent a theater or hall in the next town. She was there selling tickets and programs when the two would arrive.

Hank and Jimmie swept onstage in matching cowboy outfits—broad-brimmed white hats, yellow kerchiefs, tailored white suits, and boots with a mirror finish. Jimmie opened the show with "Good evening, ladies and gentlemen"; then Hank took over with young Jimmie coming back later for duets.

Hank was a perfectionist. Jimmie had to know his lines word perfect. His enunciation and rhythm had to be flawless; his costume spotless. Once an older boy lured Jimmie to a creek and pushed him in just before the show.

When Hank saw his wet and muddy costume, he made him parade before the crowd in a dress and then whipped him soundly.

They went to West Virginia for a few months and sang on WWVA, Wheeling. Then Hank took their savings and bought a trick horse, a tent, a portable grandstand, a truck, and a semi. With a hired band and a juggler, they hit the Canadian circuit again.

Hank did rope tricks and daredevil riding acts. At his father's cue, Jimmie would jump on the stirrup to spin a rope and sing a duet with Hank. Jimmie also assisted the juggler with a dangerous knife trick.

After a couple of years Hank sent Jimmie and Minnie home, while he tried his luck in Hollywood. The publicity men took everything he had, and he moved on to Dallas to take a job on KRLD's "Big-D Jamboree." In 1948 when Jimmie was eleven, Hank sent for his wife and son to come to Texas.

For several months the family slept with their horse, Shawnee, in the truck which Hank kept parked in front of a nightspot where he also entertained. Jimmie sang with Hank in the Roundup Club and at the Silver Spur down the street. The latter was operated by Jack Ruby who later shot Lee Harvey Oswald before television cameras.

When not assisting his father, Jimmie sat at tables with drinking patrons or danced with women customers. During the day he played hooky from school and robbed newspaper boxes downtown.

At KRLD Hank became good friends with Ernest Tubb, the "Texas Troubadour." Ernest had a son, Justin, a year older than Jimmie, and the two singers shared a common admiration for the late Jimmie Rodgers. The brakeman's widow had helped Ernest get a recording contract and had even lent him one of Jimmie Rodgers' guitars. When the Snows came along, Ernest was making money from "I'm Walking the Floor over You," "I'll Get Along Somehow," and "Take Me Back and Try Me One More Time."

Ernest had made a profession of faith and been baptized in a Baptist church at fourteen. But like so many other western singers, he had let music take the place of church attendance. Nevertheless, he would help anybody and was known to give away more money than he made. Cal Smith, another entertainer, said, "Ernest doesn't go to church anymore. But if he doesn't go to heaven, there isn't a heaven."

Ernest joined the Grand Ole Opry and brought Hank Snow to Nashville. Hank went on the WSM stage in 1950 and rocketed to fame with a railroad song which was pure vintage Jimmie Rodgers. "I'm Movin' On" remained number one for twenty-nine weeks—a record which still stands.

The Snows got a house of their own in Madison, a northern suburb, and hoped to put down roots. Jimmie brought to Tennessee all the bad habits he had learned in Texas. Now a sixth grader, he took cards and dice to school and operated his own "casino" in the schoolyard during recess. Inside, when he was supposed to be studying, he picked wallets from pockets and purses. At test time he gave his victims part of their money back for the privilege of copying their papers. Hank and Minnie didn't know their son had become an accomplished gambler, con man, and thief.

Jimmie found it easy to slip bills out of his father's billfold at night. With the money, Jimmie bought a gun and hired a taxi to ride around Nashville after school. Jimmie carried the gun in his book bag and sometimes let his classmates have a peek.

Sometimes cashing $100 bills at the lunch counter, he would wave the money around to get attention. When asked where he got the money, he would say nonchalantly, "Don't you know that my daddy is Hank Snow?" In the eighth grade they voted him "Most Unlikely to Succeed." The school authorities also caught on and booted him from one school to another.

In the early fifties, Opry entertainers had little social status in the "Athens of the South." City fathers and social snobs made jokes about hillbillies coming in from the country and sleeping in cars around the Ryman Auditorium. Some resented the Ryman's being used for the Opry. It had once been the home of grand opera, symphony orchestras, and other high-class entertainment before the country singers took over.

For Jimmie the center of everything was the Opry. It was the one place he felt he belonged, the most exciting place in town on Saturday night.

Standing in the stage wings, he heard Roy Acuff and the Smoky Mountain Boys shake the rafters with "The Wabash Cannonball." He howled at the blackface comedians, Jam-up and Honey, and at Minnie Pearl swirling her frilly skirt and shouting, "Howdeeee, I'm jist so glad to be here." He tapped his foot to Red Foley's "Peace in the Valley" and hummed behind Hank Williams' "Cold, Cold Heart." Between acts he ran around backstage with other Opry kids.

Of course Jimmie knew about the drinking and the drug problems of Hank and Red. All the Opry families did.

Hank Williams seemed to be in the worst shape. On road trips fellow entertainers would remove bottles he had hidden in his bags, refuse to let him order drinks in restaurants, and escort him to the hotel where they locked him in his room until time for the performance. He outsmarted his protectors for a while by concealing whiskey in shaving lotion and cologne bottles. When they caught on to this trick, he still found ways to get liquor. Hank's buddies were afraid he wouldn't last long, but his fans thought the immortal Hank Williams would go on forever.

The big moment came for Hank Snow on the Opry: "Ladies and gentlemen, I'm proud to present my son, Jimmie Rodgers Snow." Jimmie was still a little young, but he sang well and everybody expected he would be an

Opry member in a few years.

But Jimmie was now more interested in a neighborhood girl. Her protective parents would only permit him to take her to their Assembly of God church.

The hymns didn't affect him. He had heard entertainers sing the same songs and then head out with a woman and a bottle. But the preaching made him miserable, for a voice kept nagging, *Boy, you can't fool God. He knows all about you.*

He kept going back with the girl, thinking he could fight off the call to repent and get saved. He couldn't!

One night the preacher pleaded, "Give God a chance. Come to the altar tonight."

Jimmie twisted and squirmed, looking for some way to escape. "Come on, sinner. Come now!" The choir began singing, "Just as I am . . . I come, I come."

"Now is the hour!" the preacher shouted. "Now!"

A boy Jimmie knew put an arm around him. "Let Jesus have his way," he urged.

The next thing Jimmie knew he was kneeling and crying at the altar while the boy quoted Scripture about how Jesus had died for his sins. "Ask Jesus to save you, Jimmie," the boy encouraged.

"Jesus, take me," Jimmie cried. "Come into my heart."

People all around were shouting, "Praise the Lord!" Some were pointing and saying, "That's Hank Snow's son."

Recalling the experience, Jimmie says, "I didn't really know what was happening. I just felt different and clean all over."

Jimmie continued to attend the church for a while and then drifted away after breaking up with the girl. At seventeen he started boozing, thinking he had no chance of becoming an alcoholic like Red Foley and Hank Williams. The liquor made him feel good and snapped inhibitions.

Hank Williams was now the biggest voice in country music. "Cold, Cold Heart," "Hey, Good Lookin'," "Your Cheatin' Heart," and other records were making him a millionaire. Yet his life was spinning out of control, thanks to whiskey, drugs, and easy women. On top of this, in January 1952 he had to have back surgery. Then he fell and reinjured his back. When infection spread throughout his body, doctors, knowing his weakness for wild living, gave him only a year to live.

Audrey Williams filed for divorce. In May the decree came through, giving her a whopping financial settlement. Hank quickly remarried, repeating the ceremony onstage twice to capacity audiences in New Orleans. In December, the Opry fired him for drunkenness and irresponsibility just before it was announced that his "Jambalaya" was the top-selling record of the year.

Hank Williams must have known he was going. Riding in a car with several other performers, who were trying to keep him sobered up for a performance, he suddenly began singing "I Saw the Light." Then he looked up with sad eyes and moaned, "Minnie (Pearl), there ain't no more light for me."

He had a New Year's show date in Canton, Ohio, and hired a man to drive him there in a Cadillac. They stopped to get a shot of pain-killer for his back. After Hank became quiet, the driver stopped to see if he was all right and found him dead in the back seat. The autopsy linked his heart failure to excessive drinking.

Jimmie heard his country music friends tell about Hank and how he could move from a honky-tonk song to a spiritual—singing like a devil one minute and a saint the next. Though he used profanity freely, Hank had fined his band members a quarter each time they used the Lord's name in vain on a trip. While he didn't care for formal religion, he could get emotional talking about God and spiritual matters. Some said he must have been a be-liever, for how else could he have written "I Saw the Light" and "Mansion over the Hill-top"?

On a cold winter day, 25,000 people sought the 2,750 seats for his funeral in Montgomery, Alabama's municipal auditorium. It was a country music spectacular. Ernest Tubb sang "Beyond the Sunset"; Roy Acuff "I Saw the Light"; and Red Foley, his voice breaking, "Peace in the Valley." Four women fainted, and a fifth who fell at the foot of the casket had to be carried from the auditorium in hysterics.

In death, Hank Williams had founded a cult. His divorced wife and his widow made special personal appearances. MGM produced the movie, *Your Cheatin' Heart*, which made no mention of booze, drugs, womanizing, and his divorce. His records sold faster than ever. Ironically, the biggest seller the year after his death was "I'll Never Get out of This World Alive."

When he died, Hank Williams was only twenty-nine, just thirteen years older than Jimmie Snow, yet Jimmie saw no similarity between Hank's dissolute life-style and his own. He went right on drinking.

Hank Snow still hadn't realized what a wild life his son was leading. He encouraged Jimmie to sign up with promoter Colonel Tom Parker for show tours with Mother Maybelle and the Carter Sisters, Marty Robbins, a new country comic named Andy Griffith, and other talent. In Memphis, Colonel Parker picked up Elvis Presley, the young hip-wiggler from Mississippi. Elvis had guested on the Opry, hoping to be invited into membership. After an Opry official saw him wiggle his hips, he was told he'd be better off driving a truck. But the response of the audience to Elvis' gyrations onstage gave Colonel Parker other ideas.

The Colonel booked Elvis and Jimmie Snow together. They made a strange pair. Jimmie smoked, drank, and cursed, while Elvis abstained. He knew church songs and quoted the Bible like a preacher. But both liked girls and sex.

Jimmie saw Elvis run country, pop, and rhythm-and-blues music together with a fast beat, setting the rock-and-roll style which the Beatles and others picked up. Backed by a frenzied drum beat, the sensual crooning, howling, wailing, hip-wiggling Elvis drove teenaged girls and women into mass hysteria.

In Jacksonville, Florida, Jimmie and Elvis had to literally race for their lives across a football field, in front of a pack of screaming women and girls. The crafty Colonel had signed an unusual management contract with Elvis, giving him one-half of the singer's receipts. When he saw what he had, he dropped Jimmie and the others and took Elvis on full-time.

Having nothing better to do, Jimmie went with his father and Ernest Tubb to the annual memorial celebration they had started in Meridian, Mississippi, in honor of Jimmie Rodgers. After a few drinks, Jimmie told one of Hank Thompson's band members, "I can't sing." The musician slipped him a couple of Benzedrines for a "lift." Jimmie asked for another and another. By year's end he was hooked.

Popping pills on top of boozing, Jimmie began losing show dates. He lost interest in music and even stopped going to the Opry when home on weekends. God and church behind him, he cared only for bar hopping, hot-rodding, and picking up women. The pills and the booze helped him make it from one day to the next. Hank Snow's son had become a familiar face in every beer joint and night-club in North Nashville.

By now Hank knew all about his son, Jimmie. Phone calls had come from bars where Jimmie owed money. A policeman had come to the house on a complaint that Jimmie and some friends had gotten drunk and nailed all the furniture in a motel room to the ceiling. Jimmie, intercepting the officer in the yard, paid the damages.

Hank laid down one ultimatum after another. One night Hank followed Jimmie downtown and watched him go into a club. He slipped into a phone booth and warned the manager, "Get that underaged boy out in two minutes or I'm calling the police." The manager threw Jimmie out and he went directly to another club.

"I've taken your name off as beneficiary to my estate," Hank finally informed his only child. As Jimmie sat stunned, Hank assured him that he would always have a place to eat and sleep. "My stepfather threw me out of my home," he recalled. "I'll never do that to you."

Jimmie stalked out of the house, drove to the Army recruiting office, and enlisted without telling his parents.

On the evening of January 3, 1956, three days before he was due to report for duty, Jimmie headed for a drive-in movie. Slowing to turn left across four-lane Dickerson Road near the theater, he was hit head on by a drunk fleeing police at 105 miles per hour. The nub on the steering wheel shattered against his chest. The steering column was driven into his thigh, pushing the bone all the way through. He spent thirty-eight days in the hospital, got over 10,000 get-well letters from fans, and went home on crutches, unchanged.

He returned to the pills and the booze. Then at the fall deejay convention, he ran into some old friends from WWVA, Wheeling, West Virginia. He greeted Wilma Lee and Stoney Cooper who had just come to Nashville to join the Opry. They brought along their fifteen-year-old daughter, Carol, a beauty with long dark hair.

Upon hearing that the Coopers were to accompany his father on a show tour across Canada, Jimmie took a new interest in music. Because they were the only teenagers in the group, he and Carol spent a lot of time together. He told Carol about his experience in church. "I was really happy there for a while," he confided sincerely. "I'd sure like to get back."

For reasons he couldn't understand, his show business career began picking up after he returned. RCA offered a new recording contract. Invitations came for him to sing on the Opry. Would membership be next? Tennessee Governor Frank Clement recommended him to famed dramatics teacher, Elia Kazan. Lawrence Welk asked him to Hollywood for a television appearance. Jimmie returned home, shared his excitement with Carol Cooper, then went out and got drunk.

A week later the Coopers let him take Carol

to see *The Ten Commandments*. He was so taken with the biblical story that he saw the movie ten times. He started reading the Bible every day. He took Carol to church and she was converted.

Late one evening he sat in his bedroom with his Bible open. "I wanted to throw myself upon God's mercy," he recalls, "yet I was afraid. Afraid that if I did get saved, really saved, I would have to preach. How could a booze-hound, pill-head, and skirt-chaser like me become a preacher? It seemed impossible."

He talked to Carol about being a preacher's wife. She was agreeable.

On Wednesday night, November 27, 1957, Jimmie came home drunk again. He wobbled into his room, somehow managing not to awake his mother.

"At twenty-one I had everything the world says should make you happy," he later wrote. "Youth, money, a famous name, friends like Elvis Presley, Tommy Sands, Bill Haley. A beautiful girl who had said she would marry me. Opportunities opening to make it big on my own. Yet I had nothing and hated my wretched, miserable, empty self. I seemed to have a gift for ruining everything I touched. Booze and pills had totally enslaved me, and Dad had given up and disinherited me.

"Being cut off from Dad's money didn't hurt as much as the realization that I had shattered all his dreams for me. He had waited so long to present me as the newest member of the Grand Ole Opry. Now I was Jimmie Rodgers Snow—The Bum."

Jimmie reached into his pants' pocket and pulled out the snub-nosed Smith-and-Wesson revolver he had carried for years. This wasn't the first time he had started to kill himself. A few weeks before, he had swallowed a handful of barbiturates and failed. Then he'd tried driving his car a hundred miles an hour, intending to smash into a telephone pole. Each time he had swerved away, unable to let go.

He stuck the gun barrel in his mouth and got set to pull the trigger, but couldn't do it. Throwing the gun on the bed, he lurched toward the door. He staggered into the cold night air. Reaching the mailbox, he fell on his face, crying, "Help me, God! If you're real, help me, God!" He prayed louder and louder. Neighbors began turning on lights.

"I must have prayed an hour in the freezing cold. I would have stayed there all night, I was so desperate. But at some time, somehow, I reached out in faith to God. My mind cleared and I was filled with an overflowing peace. I knew my past had been forgiven and that my future belonged to him. Not only had God accepted me, but he was also going to use me in his service. Like Moses, I was going to be his spokesman."

He ran into the house shouting, "Mother, I've found God! I'm going to be a preacher!"

Jarred awake, Minnie Snow looked at her son and sighed, "Son, you're going to have a nervous breakdown yet."

Jimmie drove to the house of Jay Alford, the pastor of the local Assembly of God church, and woke him up. "God has saved me, Brother Alford," he announced. "He wants me to be a preacher." He and the pastor talked and prayed until almost daylight.

The pastor wanted him to attend the Assemblies of God Bible college in Springfield, Missouri. Jimmie had not finished high school but wanted to get married first. When he and Carol realized her folks were not going to consent, they eloped. Stoney and Wilma Lee, angry and hurt, talked of having the marriage annulled. Hank and Minnie Snow were also upset, but said the newlyweds could live with them until they found a place. Hank introduced them at the Opry as husband and wife.

Jimmie's pastor invited him to preach at the church. Jimmie rehearsed his sermon, based on the gospel tract, "Twelve Men and a Light," in front of his father. "Sounds good," Hank said but didn't attend the service. After Jimmie delivered the sermon, the church people hugged him and said he would make a fine preacher.

The young couple moved into a trailer. Jimmie began wondering if God really wanted him to be a preacher; perhaps he could serve God just as well as an entertainer. One night in August 1958, he prayed so loud and long that a neighbor from the adjoining trailer yelled, "Shut up and go to sleep!"

Finally Jimmie made a bargain with God,

"Lord, if you want me to preach, get me invited somewhere by the first of September."

Near the end of August a woman from the church called. "I know you and Carol love the Lord," she said. "Would both of you come and sing next Friday night at the mission I've started downtown in a trailer park? And Jimmie, would you give your testimony?" Jimmie said yes and wrote down the address: Second Avenue near the Ryman Auditorium.

When Jimmie stood up to speak, he faced an audience of twenty-two sitting in folding chairs. To his right he could see people lining up for the Opry where his father and Carol's parents would soon go onstage. While he told about his experience at the mailbox, he kept one eye on the sidewalk, hoping none of the Opry entertainers would stop to listen. He was still afraid to give up show business since he knew he could make a living from it.

In October a revival preacher named Glen Miller came to the church. One night Miller interrupted his sermon and announced, "Jimmie and Carol Snow, I have a word from the Lord for you. You are to step out on faith and trust him to provide."

Jimmie cancelled his show dates and bought a reference Bible recommended by Miller. The following Thursday night he substituted for his pastor in a revival in a little church on Trinity Lane. His mother and Maybelle Carter came to hear his first attempt at an original sermon. It was over in four minutes.

As news spread that Hank Snow's son had

become a preacher for the Assemblies of God churches, preaching invitations began coming. Jimmie bought a children's *Hurlburt's Bible Storybook* and memorized biographies of Bible characters. Eck Carter, Maybelle's husband, invited Jimmie to use his large library of Bible study books. Jimmie spent many hours there, asking Eck questions and looking up interpretations of difficult verses. He also took correspondence courses from Moody Bible Institute.

His intention was to enroll in the Assemblies of God Bible college for the fall of 1959. By summer, he had so many preaching and revival requests that he decided to postpone formal training for a year.

The pastors who invited him and Carol placed large ads in local newspapers, encouraging people to hear Hank Snow's son preach and Wilma Lee and Stoney Cooper's daughter sing. Jimmie and Carol's names were in small print under their pictures. Since their parents had no objection to the piggy-back promotion, the young couple didn't either.

In 1960 the Reverend C. M. Ward, the Assemblies' radio preacher, told their story in a booklet called "From Rock-and-Roll to a Passion for Souls." The booklet gave them a kind of official sanction among Assemblies churches. With that and their parents' fame they became celebrities in the denomination.

Jimmie never went to Bible college. For the

next six years he and Carol crisscrossed the country, holding revivals in Assembly of God churches.

Jimmie's most popular sermon dealt with rock-and-roll music, against which he took a hard line. "This music primarily appeals to the sensual nature," he said. "It takes control of the mind and opens the door to drugs and illicit sex. Don't try to tell me it doesn't. I've been there." CBS-TV filmed a sermon segment for its "Evening News" telecast. In Plant City, Florida, church youth publicly burned hundreds of rock-and-roll records.

Thousands walked the sawdust trail during Jimmie and Carol's six years of evangelistic ministry. Yet the young couple faced times of discouragement. Small churches couldn't pay enough for their expenses. They could only hope to make up the shortfall in larger crusades. This didn't always work out, for in some churches the pastor and the treasurer would skim the cream off a large offering given for Jimmie and Carol and use it to pay local church bills.

Phony, fraudulent evangelists were more disillusioning. One revival preacher told Jimmie, "I don't need divine power. I can anoint myself and do the job." Another displayed pickled frogs and animal embryos in jars of formaldehyde and claimed they were demons he had cast out of people. This man died in a drunken stupor. Another rigged his microphone so he could give an electrical charge to persons as they came through a healing line for prayer.

One revivalist chided Jimmie, "You know all the tricks of show business. You're a fool for not making a hundred thousand a year."

"If I want to go that route," Jimmie replied, "I'll go back to the music business."

Jimmie and Carol's first child, Vanessa, was born September 19, 1962. Jimmie was away in a revival in St. Louis. Three weeks later mother and daughter joined him on the evangelistic circuit. They put the baby in a bassinet on the platform and held the services.

Every month or so they went home for a few days. On Saturday nights they visited friends backstage at the Opry. Here Jimmie frequently had opportunities to share the gospel.

In the early sixties when Marijohn Wilkin was struggling to find her way back to God, the Christian witness among country entertainers in Nashville was weak. Even those who wanted to be loyal to their church could not attend services regularly. They were performing in some distant city, at least every other Saturday night, and could hardly get back to Nashville in time. At home, Saturday night performances at the Opry kept them up late. Because almost all were from out of town, few had local church connections. For their part, most churches seemed neither to know nor to care about reaching the entertainers and the songwriters.

Jimmie Snow, more than any other preacher in Nashville, understood the peculiarities and the job situations of country music people. He knew them as a member of the "family" with their marital infidelities, divorces, boozing, and drug use. He believed many wanted to know God if only they could find someone who could point the way to the "Light" about which Hank Williams had sung so eloquently.

In 1962 Jimmie and Carol were home between revivals when the phone jangled them awake early one morning. "Praise the Lord!" a deep growl shouted in Jimmie's ear. He knew that sandpaper voice but couldn't place the name.

"Praise the Lord! Son, don't you know your old pal, Tex Tyler?"

T. Texas Tyler, of course. Jimmie's roommate on a number of old show tours. One of the truly great western artists who had sung in many western movies, he was in a class with Gene Autry, Roy Rogers, Bob Wills, and Eddie Arnold. Billed as "the man with a million friends," Tex had scored with "Remember Me" in the forties—which became his theme song—and had then hit the early fifties with "A Deck of Cards," which sent him to Carnegie Hall.

The last time Jimmie remembered being with Tex was for an afternoon matinee in El Paso. Afterwards, Tex had gone back to their room and run into the arms of waiting police. They booked him for smuggling drugs across the Mexican border and threw him into a padded cell. Tex never made the second performance.

"I just had to call and tell you I've been saved, son," Tex said over the phone. "You won't believe it, but I'm preaching just like you. Praise the Lord!"

Tex told of how after the arrest in El Paso he had gone from bad to worse, popping pills and boozing. Besides the kid preacher, Jimmie Snow, he had one other old friend who he knew was a genuine Christian. This was Carl "Deacon" Moore, a veteran deejay, music promoter, and hotel man. Deacon and Tex had played golf together every time they could get together, and Deacon usually managed to get in a word for the Lord. More than once he told Tex, "Buddy, think how much influence you could be in turning people to God if you should get saved." Tex had always brushed off Deacon's witness. Then he became desperate and called his friend.

"Deacon, I'm in trouble. I think I may kill myself. Can you come and see me?"

Tex lived in California's San Gabriel Valley, and Deacon was south of Los Angeles at Huntington Beach. "I'm comin', Tex," he promised. "Hang on 'til I get there."

Deacon found Tex drunk, running around the house, and screaming, "I'm going crazy! What am I gonna do?"

Deacon wasted no time. "Get down here on your knees. Repeat after me, 'God, I'm no good. I've tried everything else in the world and nothing has worked. It's either you, Lord, or nothing. If you can change my life, now's the time.'"

Tex fell on his knees, roaring drunk, and got up as sober as a preacher in a pulpit.

Tex lived only a few more years, but he proclaimed the gospel until the day he died.

It was Tex Tyler's call which made Jimmie Snow feel God could do something among the country musicians in Nashville. Perhaps God wanted him and Carol to start a church which would appeal to country music people, making them feel at home and be themselves. It would be a place where they could find the "peace in the valley" for which Red Foley was still searching.

However, a string of revival commitments was ahead. Jimmie didn't know how, when, or where to begin. He would talk with Carol and maybe an Assembly of God pastor or two. And pray.

Later that same year they were home again. Down at the Opry Jimmie talked with Patsy Cline, then the biggest female star in the country music world. The year before, *Billboard* had named her the top female artist of the year. There was talk that she might succeed the reigning "Queen of Country Music," Kitty Wells.

One of her biggest hits was "I Fall to Pieces." Now she was telling the Reverend Jimmie Snow, "I'm not happy. I know I need to get right with God."

"Well, the way is open, Patsy," he said. "Jesus died for you and wants to forgive you.

Would you like to turn to him now?"

"Not now," she demurred. "I'm not ready yet."

"I'll pray for you," Jimmie promised as Patsy hurried onstage for her next show.

Once again Jimmie felt the urge to start a church in Nashville.

4

Peace in the Valley

Patsy Cline's real name was Virginia Patterson Hensley. A pretty, apple-cheeked girl with an open smile, she had come from a poor family in Winchester, Virginia. Dropping out of high school to work to support her parents, she sang during the evenings in churches, honky-tonks, and even on street corners.

In 1948 when Patsy was sixteen, she drove to Nashville with her sister and a family friend who wanted to get her an audition. They slept in the car and on park benches and ate peanut butter sandwiches for meals. Patsy sang for Roy Acuff, who then let her perform on his radio program on WSM. The station management wanted her to stay over to audition as a possible regular on Roy's show. But she had to leave because they had barely enough money for gas to get home.

For the next five years Patsy sang with the

Melody Playboys around Winchester. In 1953 she married Gerald Cline. The stormy union lasted only three years. During that time Patsy's singing reputation grew, and she guested on the "Ozark Jubilee," the "Jimmy Dean Show," and several other regional television programs.

In 1957 she married Charlie Dick, a local Winchester man who had served in Korea.

Her song, "Walkin' after Midnight," which she sang on the "Arthur Godfrey Show," put her on the record charts. But when she became pregnant, she wanted simply to settle down with Charlie and enjoy a quiet life.

Charlie told her not to waste her talent, and they moved to Nashville. She recorded "I Fall to Pieces"; thanks to her warm, throbbing voice, the song became the number one country record in 1960.

Patsy was a soft touch for younger entertainers trying to make it in the business. One she befriended was Loretta Lynn, a coal miner's daughter from Kentucky, perhaps because their backgrounds were so similar. Loretta and her husband, Mooney, had also slept in their car and lived off sandwiches during their first trip to Nashville. Loretta's career moved faster than Patsy's. The Wilburn Brothers, Doyle and Teddy, put Loretta on their syndicated television show and secured her a recording contract.

Some said Loretta was trying to be another Patsy Cline, but Patsy didn't seem to mind. She taught Loretta how to walk onstage, how to play to a crowd, and how to walk off. Patsy often went to Loretta's house with an extra blouse or skirt. "I was out shopping and bought one of these for myself. I just knew you'd like one, too," Patsy would say. The two became best friends.

In 1961 Patsy, then only twenty-nine and the mother of two young children, was critically injured in a near-fatal car accident. She was in the hospital almost six months and survived. Loretta visited her and joked about Patsy's hit record, "I Fall to Pieces." A week after leaving the hospital, Patsy recorded another hit song, "Crazy."

Patsy was apparently going through another valley when she and Jimmie Snow talked backstage at the Opry. Jimmie had to leave for another revival but encouraged Patsy to attend the suburban Madison Assembly of God church which he and Carol attended. She went to the altar there early in 1963 and told friends that she had found God and was happy.

On another return home, Jimmie talked with Lloyd ("Cowboy") Copas, one of the best-liked cowboy singers on the Opry. Lean and lanky, Cowboy had begun singing on the radio and playing county fairs at fourteen. He joined the Opry in 1946 and made a hit with "My Filipino Baby."

Jimmie knew Cowboy and his family well. Jimmie and Cowboy's son, Gary, had run around together before Jimmie's conversion. Randy Hughes, Cowboy's pilot son-in-law and the road manager for Patsy Cline and Billy

Walker, was also Jimmie's good friend.

Talking with Cowboy about spiritual matters was hard because he lived a better moral life than many active church members Jimmie knew. Cowboy was courteous; he said he already belonged to a church but just didn't want to get closely involved.

One of Jimmie's favorite country music couples was Harold ("Hawkshaw") Hawkins and Jean Shepard Hawkins. The tall, amiable Hawkshaw, forty-three, was an old friend of the Snow family from West Virginia days; his wife, Jean, was a ranch girl from Oklahoma. Both were doing well in country music. Jean usually came to hear Jimmie preach when he was holding revivals in Nashville. Hawkshaw was always "going to come" but never got around to it.

Hawkshaw sang in a deep-voiced western style. His early recording of "Sunny Side of the Mountain" had already become a country classic. His distinctive stage garb was a black jacket with the hawk emblem on back, symbolizing his nickname.

When Jimmie came to visit, he and Jean were expecting their second child in three weeks. In a talkative mood, Hawkshaw said, "Jimmie [none of the entertainers ever called Jimmie "Reverend"], I'm going to tell you something nobody in Nashville knows. When I was a boy back in West Virginia, God called me to be an evangelist like you. But I loved the music business so much that I ran out of that church and never returned."

"How's your life been since?" Jimmie asked.

"I've gone higher than I ever dreamed. But I've always known something important was missing."

"You know what it is," Jimmie reminded him.

"Yes, I've left the Lord out of my life."

"Why don't you turn your life over to him? He'll show you what's really best."

"I intend to do that," Hawkshaw said resolutely. "Cowboy, Patsy Cline, Billy Walker, Dottie West, and I are going on a tour. Tex Ritter was going, but something came up and I'm taking his place. Our last show will be a benefit for the family of Cactus Jack in Kansas City. You remember our old deejay buddy who was killed in a car accident?

"Well, when I get home, I promise you, I'll be in church the next Sunday." Hawkshaw stood up and circled the date on a wall calendar: March 9, 1963.

The evening before they left, Patsy Cline came over to help Loretta Lynn hang drapes. Patsy had just replaced Kitty Wells as number one female singer, and Loretta had been voted "Most Promising Singer." "You're going to be number one next year," Patsy predicted.

"Don't be silly," Loretta argued. "You'll be number one for years to come."

After hanging the drapes, they went to Patsy's house to hear some tapes. As they listened, Patsy embroidered a tablecloth while her little boy, Randy, played on a rocking horse nearby. Before Loretta left about midnight, Patsy gave her a red nightgown, and they set a date to go shopping when the group returned from Kansas City.

Cowboy's son-in-law, Randy Hughes, flew Patsy, Cowboy, and Hawkshaw in his private plane. Dottie West and her husband went by car; Billy Walker flew commercial. The Monday after the show in Kansas City dawned cold, stormy, and rainy. Randy suggested they delay their flight.

While Dottie and Patsy breakfasted together in the hotel coffee shop, Patsy seemed anxious to get back to her babies. "Why don't you ride home with us?" Dottie suggested. "No telling when your plane will go. Let the men fly. Billy Walker can take your place." Patsy agreed to do that and left to pack.

But when Patsy returned to the lobby, her mind was changed. "Baby, y'all go on. Even if we don't take off for a few hours, I can still beat you."

Dottie kept urging her to come in the car. "No, go on," Patsy insisted. "I'll be all right. If it's my time to go, I'll go."

On Tuesday the airport was locked in with fog, but flights were cleared by midafternoon. Billy Walker boarded a commercial plane, while Patsy, Cowboy, and Hawkshaw climbed into the single-engine Comanche with Randy.

The flight to the Tennessee border went fairly well. They refueled, as planned, in Dyersburg, Tennessee. Since thunderstorms were then rolling through the area, the Dyersburg tower advised them to stay on the ground.

They talked about renting a car but finally decided to fly through the storms anyway since they were so close to Nashville. They took off from Dyersburg at 6:07 P.M.

Wednesday morning at 4:00 A.M. (3:00 A.M. Nashville time), Patsy's brother Sam answered the phone in Winchester, Virginia. "I heard on the radio that a plane crashed with Patsy on board," a friend reported.

"Are you pulling a joke?" Sam replied angrily. "Patsy isn't on a plane."

Patsy's mother grabbed the phone. "Hold it. Patsy *was* on a plane."

Later that morning in Nashville, Loretta Lynn began wondering why Patsy hadn't been in touch. They were supposed to go shopping. Just then, Patsy's booking agent called and said, "They all died in a plane crash."

"Baloney! Patsy and me are goin' shoppin' this morning." Loretta didn't believe it. Then she turned on the radio and heard the horrible truth.

Reports of a plane in trouble had started coming in around seven the evening before, about the time the group had been scheduled to land in Nashville. People told of hearing first a motor backfiring, then a roar, and finally nothing. Search crews combed the dense woods in the immediate area. About 6:00 A.M. a farmer and his son located the crash site on a ridge.

Airplane parts and bodies were strewn along a 250-foot stretch near which the plane had apparently sliced the top of an oak. Even before finding purses and wallets, the rescuers identified the occupants. A white belt emblazoned with "Hawkshaw Hawkins," lay beside a black-and-white cowboy boot. Two feet away, someone found a guitar neck labeled "Hawkshaw." A soft, gold slipper was identified as Patsy's. A *Flyer's Bible* was found under torn clothing. A hand-printed song titled "Boo Hoo Hoo" cried out the sad ending.

Adding pathos to the tragedy, record producer Don Pierce showed reporters Cowboy Copas's newly released album, "Beyond the Sunset." Besides the title song, it included, "Family Reunion," "The Wreck on the Highway," and "A Picture from Life's Other Side."

Family members were notified; funerals were scheduled. Cowboy, Randy, and Hawkshaw were buried in Nashville's Forest Lawn Cemetery. Patsy's body remained with her family and close friends at her home for two days. Then on Friday afternoon, her pastor, Jay Alford, led a prayer service after which her remains were sent in a gold-trimmed casket to Winchester for burial. A simple, bronze plaque, placed over her grave, read:

VIRGINIA H. (PATSY CLINE) DICK
1932–1963
DEATH CANNOT KILL WHAT NEVER DIES

The gloom that had fallen over the country music community intensified when Opry star Jack Anglin was killed in an auto wreck on the way to Patsy's service in Virginia. Jack had been the singing partner of Johnny Wright,

Kitty Wells' husband, and a close friend of those who had died in the plane crash.

In Nashville, country music fans streamed into Forest Lawn Memorial Gardens for a week. At times the line of cars was five miles long. Mountains of flowers covered the graves, both in Nashville and in Winchester. During the week scores of radio stations broadcast songs by Cowboy, Hawkshaw, Patsy, and Jack Anglin.

The Saturday night memorial service at 8:30 in the Ryman Auditorium was something people never forgot:

"What do we say when we lose such friends?" Opry manager, Ott Devine, said. "We can reflect upon their contributions to all of us through entertainment and upon their acts of charity and of love. We can think of the pleasure they brought to the lives of millions and take some comfort in knowing that they found fulfillment in the time allotted to them.

"We can share the sorrow of their families and appreciate their loss, not only to WSM and the Grand Ole Opry but also to their associates, to the music industry, and especially to all of you . . . their friends. There is a great significance that Patsy, Cowboy, Hawkshaw, and Randy were returning from a performance staged to help others when they lost their own lives. They will never be forgotten.

"All of their friends standing with me here tonight . . . know that it is impossible to put into words our thoughts, our feelings, our love. And so we ask that you in our audience please stand

and join us for a moment of silent prayer in tribute to them. . . .

". . . Thank you. Patsy, Cowboy, Hawkshaw, Jack, and Randy never walked on this stage without a smile. They would want us to keep on smiling . . . and to recall the happier occasions. I feel that I can speak for all of them when I say . . . let's continue in the tradition of the Grand Ole Opry."

The Jordainaires closed the tribute by singing "How Great Thou Art." Roy Acuff struck up a fast fiddle tune for the show had to go on. Minnie Pearl was next.

Standing in the wings, Minnie motioned to Roy for another minute to compose herself. When he waved her on, Minnie was still wiping her eyes as she rushed out onstage and shouted her familiar down-home greeting, "Howdeeee, I'm jist so proud to be here!" A sea of handkerchiefs fluttered before her. A moment later she had the audience howling with laughter.

When Minnie reached the solace of the wings, she burst into tears again. "Oh, Lord," she cried, "we lost some good friends!"

On March 29, 1963, Texas Ruby Fox, a member of the Opry since 1933, died in a trailer fire.

Then it was "Gentleman" Jim Reeves.

Jim might have been a professional baseball player, had an arm injury in the St. Louis Cardinals' training camp not cut short his career. Turning to music, he'd made it big with "Mexican Joe," the number one song in 1953, and "Bimbo."

Jim used to hold the mike right on his mouth to give the effect that he was singing to one person. His soft sound, similar to Eddie Arnold's, gave a touch of velvet that made country music acceptable to those who didn't like the high, fast songs of Hank Williams, Faron Young, Webb Pierce, and others. At the time of his death Jim was perhaps the most popular international star on the Opry.

On July 31, 1964, Jim and Dean Manuel, his road manager-pianist, were flying back from Batesville, Arkansas. Just twenty miles south of Nashville, their plane got caught in a thunderstorm over the affluent Brentwood community and crashed in a wooded area. At the peak of his career, Jim was just twenty days short of his forty-first birthday.

Many country music luminaries had homes in Brentwood. Marty Robbins heard the plane's engine sputtering but had no idea his friends were in trouble. After it was confirmed that Jim and Manuel had crashed, their colleagues joined in the search. Eddie Arnold scoured the area in a jeep. Carl Smith brought riding horses. Minnie Pearl, Stonewall Jackson, and Marijohn Wilkin, along with record company executives, deejays, and many others in the music business, stayed in the woods all night.

By Saturday the crowds were so large that the police had to make radio broadcasts insisting people stay away. Tears and tension pervaded the Opry that night, and many entertainers requested prayer for Jim and Dean. The wreckage was finally found the next day just fifty yards from a home. Both men were dead in the mangled wreckage.

This tragedy again plunged the country music fraternity into mourning. Massive crowds attended memorial services in Nashville and Jim's burial in his native Carthage, Texas. Near his grave, Jim's widow, Mary, set aside a two-acre memorial park with a life-sized statue of the singer standing on a monument. Workmen constructed a winding sidewalk leading to the monument and the gravesite. Part of the sidewalk was shaped like a guitar on which were inscribed the dates of Jim's birth and death and the words:

GENTLEMAN: JIM   PRODUCER: GOD

Jim Reeves and Jimmie Snow had been good friends as a result of doing a lot of show tours together. Jim and his wife, Mary, had also lived just behind the Snows in Madison. Now in little over a year Jim was the seventh member of the country music family of Nashville to die. More than ever, Jimmie felt God pulling him out of evangelism and urging him to start a church in town to reach many of the show business personalities.

Talking to an official of the Assemblies of God, Jimmie learned that the denomination ruled no new church could be built within three miles of another Assembly church. Also, a new church had to have twenty-one members before the denomination would charter it.

While Jimmie and Carol were driving around looking for possible sites, another Opry friend, Ira Louvin, died tragically. He and his brother Charlie had been famous for their songs, "Weapon of Prayer" and "The Family Who Prays."

The Snows finally found a four-acre site on Dickerson Road between two of Jimmie's old drinking hangouts. With $1,500 saved from their six years in evangelism, they put up $600 for a ninety-day option. The remainder was used for renting 500 chairs, an organ, and a public address system. Jimmie planned on preaching nightly for a month and then inviting new converts to form the new church.

Meanwhile, he and Carol made radio and television appearances, and the newspapers ran feature stories on them. Opry friends came to sing during the evening services. "Decisions for Christ" were made almost every night.

Closing out the month the last Saturday night in September 1965, Jimmie announced that services for the new church would be held the following morning. He anticipated at least a hundred people, but only ten people came, including himself and his wife.

Discouraged and ready to quit, Jimmie talked to his pastor, Jay Alford. "Try it a few more Sundays," Alford urged.

By the end of October, they had twenty-three members, enough for a charter. The name, "Evangel Temple," was chosen. "We want it to be a center of evangelism," Jimmie said.

The month's offering was just enough to pay

for the tent rental with a few dollars left for lights and heat. But it wasn't enough to pay a pastor's salary, let alone church property, and the option to buy was running out.

Having long been back in Hank's good graces, Jimmie stopped by to see his father.

"Are you serious about this church?" Hank called to Jimmie on his way out.

"Yes," Jimmie assured him. "We have twenty-three members and attendance is picking up."

"How much is the price of the property where you're meeting?"

"I put $600 on the option. The balance is $39,400."

Hank wasted no words. "OK, I'll lend you that amount. When the church is able, it can pay me back over a four-year period. Without interest."

Jimmie was overwhelmed. After all, Hank had never even been to hear him preach! "Yes, sir, thank you very much!" was all Jimmie could say.

They bought the property and Jimmie found an Assembly preacher-contractor from Memphis, who offered to arrange for $75,000 in church bonds and supervise construction. The idea was for the church to serve as the general contractor and that way save money. When the preacher asked Jimmie what he wanted in the building, Jimmie said, "Good acoustics, and a floor sloping toward the pulpit like in a theater. And make the sanctuary wide, instead of long, to create a sense of closeness."

The church approved the plans which were

drawn. Bonds were printed at 6 percent interest in denominations of $250 to $1,000. Now Jimmie had to sell them.

He immediately began calling on his entertainer friends in their offices, homes, and backstage at the Opry. Johnny Cash was caught at the Municipal Auditorium when he and June were getting ready to go onstage for a show. Johnny listened courteously as Jimmie explained the bond issue. "We'll take $4,000," Johnny pledged. Other entertainers bought more bonds until the entire issue was sold.

The building was half up when subcontractors began calling about unpaid bills. The preacher-contractor had the money from the bonds and was supposed to have kept the payments current. When Jimmie called him, he promised to take care of the subs.

But the bills went unpaid. When the church demanded an accounting from the man, he replied that his house had burned, along with all the building records.

With the building unfinished and the church owing $23,000, all the little group could do was pay and pray and work. By working on their church practically round the clock and by sacrificial giving, the small congregation paid off the debt. By 1968 attendance was up to 200, however, and the church was able to make payents to Hank, who was giving as much back to the church as they were paying him!

One of the first country music couples to start attending regularly was Lefty and Alice Frizzell. The son of a Texas oil driller, Lefty had had four songs in the "Top Ten" in one year. With his resonant tenor voice, Lefty could stretch "always" into six syllables when he sang his trademark song, "Always Late." Lefty listened attentively to Jimmie at the church but withstood every invitation to accept Christ. Lefty's wife, Alice, became a Christian, however, and later a loyal member of Evangel Temple.

Alice Frizzell later brought Dot Kilgore to church. Dot's husband, Merle, had written "Ring of Fire," which Johnny Cash was taking to the top. Dot and Merle were having marital problems at the time, probably because of Merle's heavy drinking. Then Dot accepted Christ at Evangel Temple, but Merle never came through. Their marriage later broke up.

The first big performer to join Evangel Temple was Billy Walker. Jimmie had known Billy since Dallas days when Billy and Hank Snow worked together on the "Big D Jamboree." The tall Texan, with the open, honest face, had literally gone from rags to riches.

The seventh of eight children from a poor West Texas farm family, Billy remembers the night his mother died: "I was only four and still sleeping in the baby crib because there wasn't anywhere else to sleep. The crying woke me up and I asked, 'What's wrong?' They said, 'Momma died.' I went into the next room and saw them tying Momma's feet together. She had died in childbirth."

Billy's father went to work in the oil fields,

and a black woman took care of the children for a couple of years. Then when Billy was six, he and his two brothers were put in the Methodist Orphans Home in Waco. The matrons often whipped the children. When Billy and his brothers tried to run away, they were caught and beaten until the blood flowed.

When their father remarried, he brought the family together in Clovis, New Mexico. The elder Walker loved gospel quartet singing and took Billy to singing conventions. As a result, Billy became interested in a music career. His first public singing was in a gospel quartet with his father, stepmother, and a family friend.

At fifteen Billy had his own show on KICA, Clovis. Later he worked as a front man introducing Hank Thompson onstage. Then Billy married a Texas girl and was hired for the "Big D Jamboree." His manager put a Lone Ranger mask on him and billed him "The Traveling Texan, the Masked Singer of Country Songs." In 1951 he scored his first big hit with "Anything Your Heart Desires." He would have twenty-six recordings in the "Top Ten" during the next twenty years.

From Dallas Billy moved to the "Louisiana Hayride" where he worked with Hank Williams. One night Hank told him, "Billy, I want to get my life straightened out. I'm gonna go to the Caribbean and come back a better person." Hank never did. Billy was with Hank the night Hank repeated his marriage ceremony to his second wife onstage. At that time Hank had less than six months to live.

The "Ozark Jubilee" with Red Foley in Springfield was next. Billy and Red became close friends. Billy knew about Red's drinking and heavy guilt, but at that time he didn't know how to help Red.

Billy joined the Opry in 1960. He also recorded a smash hit called "Charlie's Shoes." When he met preacher Jimmie Snow, he had a comfortable bank account, four beautiful daughters, a home near the golf course, and all the bookings he could handle.

Billy and Jimmie met for lunch at Shoney's restaurant in Madison. As they talked, Billy confided that his family seldom went to church except on Easter. "My grandfather was a Methodist minister," Billy recalled. "When I was about fourteen, I accepted the Lord. But I got away from God after I started singing on the radio." Jimmie had heard it all before. So many country entertainers had gone the path of Billy Walker.

"Jimmie, I've got success, money, everything the world thinks it takes to make you happy. But I'm in misery. I know there has to be something more than this."

Then Jimmie gave Billy his testimony. "If God can help me, I know he can help you."

"Just tell me how," Billy almost begged.

So in a booth at Shoney's, Jimmie led Billy to spiritual renewal. Like Marijohn Wilkin, he returned to the God of his childhood. He became a member of Evangel Temple and told Jimmie, "There are a lot of others like me. We've got to help them find Jesus."

One of the friends Billy wanted most to help was Red Foley. "Mr. Country Music," as Red had recently been called by *Newsweek*, was now perhaps the best loved and the most enduring of all the country artists. Since coming on the "WLS (Chicago) Barn Dance" in 1930, Red had had dozens of hits. He also had no known enemies; saint and sinner alike loved him.

When Red sang "Jesus Loves Me," "Amazing Grace," "I Know Who Holds Tomorrow," "In the Shelter of His Arms," "Hold Thou My Hand," or his all-time favorite, "Peace in the Valley," you could almost hear angel wings fluttering and the bells of heaven ringing.

In 1967 at the age of fifty-seven, Red was voted into the Country Music Hall of Fame along with deceased Jim Reeves. Although his red hair was lighter and his face showed wrinkles, it seemed he would go on forever, making people laugh and cry. But those close to him wondered how much more drinking, chain-smoking, and nightly road shows his body could take. Red said he had to keep going. "I need every dollar I can make," he told friends.

Red's son-in-law, Pat Boone, was now climbing the golden stairs in Hollywood. Perhaps it was just as well that Red didn't know that Pat and daughter Shirley's marriage was falling apart. Pat, who had pastored a church in Texas for a year and was known for his Mr. Clean, white-buck shoes image, was breaking Shirley's heart.

Partying, drinking with the "beautiful people," and then attending church on Sunday, Pat had become a first-class hypocrite in Shirley's eyes. She tried to help him see where he was heading, but he kept making excuses about balancing religion with the real world. Shirley developed such an emotional reaction to Pat that she felt nauseous whenever he tried to either hold her hand or kiss her.

Their church taught that the supernatural work of God on earth had ended with the death of the apostles. California businessman George Otis assured them that they could experience spiritual power. They could actually know God, walk in fellowship with him, and sense the presence and the power of the Holy Spirit. "God is alive today and can make you alive if you will yield to him," George said.

Shirley took Otis' suggestion to "simply surrender yourself to the Lord" and found new direction and power for herself during the summer of 1968. Pat continued to struggle for several more months.

During this time Shirley's father, Red Foley, was to perform at Disneyland in Anaheim, California. Pat and Shirley took their children to see him. To the delight of the audience, Red had his grandchildren join him in singing "John Brown's Flivver Had a Puncture in Its Tire." Afterwards the family enjoyed a good time together laughing over old times and recalling some of Red's old movies with Tex Ritter.

Pat always enjoyed telling about the scene in which Red had gotten shot and, limping on

94

one leg, had staggered off into the bushes. He had come back on camera a little later, still limping, but on the *other* leg. Red laughed heartily. He had long ago forgiven Pat for eloping with his daughter. Sadly, neither could help the other spiritually at that time.

On September 19 Red Foley, Billy Walker, and several other Opry members went to Terre Haute, Indiana, to do a police benefit show at the Scottish Rite Auditorium. They did a Wednesday afternoon matinee for 900 children. Red closed his act with the lively "Clap Your Hands." Then the sponsors took the troupe out for food and drinks. Red noticed that Billy was trying to beg off the liquor.

Back at the auditorium, Red went to Billy's dressing room. "Say, I've noticed that you're different, Billy. What happened?"

Billy related how he had been converted as a fourteen-year-old boy in Texas but had strayed away when he got into the music world. "I had to find out the hard way, Red, that success and money aren't everything."

"I know that," Red interjected.

Then Billy told how he had prayed with Jimmie Snow in the booth at Shoney's. "I asked the Lord to forgive me and I turned my life over to God, Red. Things sure have been different since then."

Red began telling Billy the pattern of his life. "I've done an awful lot of things for which I'm sorry and which I can't forget. I carry this heavy burden everywhere I go. When I go out onstage and make folks laugh and when I sing the hymns, the burden is still there. What can I do, Billy?"

Billy had a good idea what was worrying Red the most, but he didn't probe. "Red," he said, placing a comforting hand on his friend's shoulder, "have you thought about asking the Lord to forgive you, to come into your heart, and take that burden?"

Red brushed a hand through hair that was growing thin and sandy with age. He was now fifty-eight. "I've done an awful lot of things I regret."

"We all have, but the Lord is merciful and he'll forgive if you'll just ask him. You know he cared enough to die for your sins on the cross."

Red started sobbing, not an unusual thing for the man who could cry easily and make an audience cry. "OK, Billy, I'm ready. I mean it. I'm ready. Will you have a prayer with me?"

Red and Billy knelt in the dressing room while the audience waited. "Oh, Lord," Red sobbed, "you know how much I want to live a different life. Lord, you know I can't do it myself. Lord, forgive me. Come into my heart and help me. Please, Lord. I give it all over to you."

After Billy closed in prayer, they joined the others for the show. Red put on the same marvelous performance as always. He sang "Old Shep," which always brought the tears. Next came a recitation about a black couple whose dead baby was at the altar; the preacher who was conducting the funeral service was telling them that their baby was home with God.

Then Red ended with "Peace in the Valley." He left the audience still in tears.

Red walked offstage to talk with Billy. "Old pal, I want to tell you I've never sung that song like I sang it tonight. There's peace in the valley for me. That's for real."

The next day about midmorning, Red was found dead on his back in bed. A United Airlines ticket for the 2:57 P.M. Thursday afternoon flight to Nashville lay nearby.

Sally Foley, Red's wife, had been waiting at the Nashville airport. When Red didn't arrive as scheduled, she called the motel and was referred to the sheriff's office. He gave her the sad news.

The autopsy showed that Clyde Julian ("Red") Foley had died of "massive, acute pulmonary edema," which Coroner Gorden Franke defined as water-logged lungs. The doctor detected no abnormalities of the heart. He remarked that microscopic degrees of changes in the arteries had evidently caused an irregular heart rhythm which could have caused the lungs to fill up. "It is not unusual for a person to be feeling all right," he said, "and to be stricken without warning a few hours later."

The Nashville country music community was again plunged into mourning. Ralph Emery, WSM's top radio deejay, played nothing but Red Foley records on his program, "Opry Stars." "Red gave me my biggest break," Emery said over the air. "I admired him a great deal as so many others did." Many Opry personalities cried when they heard the news.

Minnie Pearl seemed to sum up the feelings of everyone: "He was one of the dearest friends I ever had."

Red's funeral and burial services were held at 2:00 P.M. the following Sunday. Over 2,000, including all the big names from the Opry and country music in Nashville, overflowed the church in Madison where his black-veiled widow, Sally, the former nightclub singer, sat with her son, two daughters, and two step-daughters. Pat Boone was there with Shirley and his brother, Nick. Red's aged parents came from Kentucky along with many other relatives.

Dr. Ira North read Psalm 23:

The Lord is my shepherd; I shall not want....
Yea, though I walk through the valley of the
shadow of death, I will fear no evil. ...

Then the Jordainaires sang the song which Red had made famous:

There will be peace in the valley some day....
There'll be no sadness, no sorrow, no trouble....
There will be peace in the valley for me.

The preacher stood up again. "You don't weep alone," he assured the grieving family. "Isn't it wonderful to have so many friends who care? And that is really what it is all about today. All of us here are trying to say, simply that we care."

Then North quoted from one of Red's recitations:

Just remember that when you take the last breath and go to the Great Beyond, all your belongings, all your earthly possessions will then belong to someone else. But everything that you are and everything that you have been will be yours forever.

At the graveside service, the four daughters hovered close to Sally Foley. Pat Boone, still struggling to find spiritual victory, noticed that Shirley was fully composed and steadying her stepmother. Remembering the stormy past of the Foley family and the sad death of Shirley's mother, he knew that his wife was being undergirded with a power beyond herself.

The preacher gave the customary prayer of commitment. Then Sally Foley, in the most moving gesture of the day, took a single red rose and placed it gently beside the grave. As Red's body was slowly lowered into the ground, his family and friends turned away sadly.

A couple of years later when Billy Walker saw Shirley Boone, they talked about her father. "There's something I should tell you," Billy said. Then he recounted the experience in Fort Wayne between shows and the prayers in the dressing room. "Your daddy died with peace," he assured her. "He had the same peace you and I have in the Lord."

5

Stars Reborn

By 1968 Evangel Temple, only three years old, had become known as the church for country music personalities. It was also the fastest growing church in Nashville.

Country music people loved and trusted Jimmie and Carol Snow as insiders. Jimmie, who preached the old-time gospel in a modern style, knew the language of country music. Carol Snow could make the organ talk and the choir move. A string band with cymbals and drums kept toes tapping.

The services were never programmed. Anyone could sing or testify, although Jimmie was careful to keep things from turning into a circus. An exciting freshness of spiritual power made church something to look forward to for many.

Six to eight persons, many from the country music community, were converted there every week.

There was Elaine Walker, for example, the daughter of Ernest Tubb. She was married to Wayne Walker, who had written many honky-tonk songs. Jimmie and Elaine had played together as kids backstage at the Opry. She had known him before and after his conversion experience at the mailbox.

The Walkers' son attended Vacation Bible School. Elaine went to see him perform at the graduation exercises and stayed to accept Christ. Thereafter she became a loyal member of Evangel Temple.

Barbara Miller, the wife of songwriter Eddie Miller, was also converted. Eddie had come to a Sunday afternoon "sing" at the church. Their daughter Pam's gospel song melted his heart. He stayed for the evening services and rushed to the altar when Jimmie gave the invitation to follow Jesus.

The next morning Eddie raced up the stairs to see his good friend, Biff Collie, who had an office in the same building. Biff, a veteran deejay and country music program producer for a network, had come to the Lord a few years before in a Southern Baptist church in Monterey Park, California. Biff had been witnessing to Eddie for several years. T. Tex Tyler, another old buddy, had also been telling Eddie that Christ could set him free from the bottle.

"Gotta tell you something, Biff," Eddie shouted. "Gotta tell you that the Lord changed my life yesterday. I went to church and heard my little girl sing. The Lord spoke to me and said, 'This is your time, boy.' I couldn't wait to get to that altar. I thought Jimmie Snow was going to preach for two months."

"Well, praise God!" Biff declared. "This is really good news."

"Yeah, and I've thrown out all my bottles. Now I've got to rewrite all my songs."

Two days later Biff and Eddie heard that Tex Tyler was dying from cancer. They phoned Tex and Eddie told him about the miracle in his life. "I can go now, Eddie," Tex said joyfully. "Ever since I was saved, I dreamed it would happen to you."

Eddie Miller's big song had been "Please Release Me." After finding Christ, he wrote, "Please Release Me from My Sins." He and his daughter also wrote several gospel songs based on sermons they heard Jimmie Snow preach. "Crumbs from the Table" was inspired by a message on the rich man and Lazarus. "The Last Altar Call" was based on Jimmie's invitation to accept Christ.

After an era of honky-tonk fever, country gospel began climbing the record charts. Jimmie felt that it was time to talk with WSM about a broadcast ministry of the church. WSM had hosted the Grand Ole Opry since 1925 and was now king of all the country music stations.

WSM's Channel 4 Television had one of the largest viewing audiences in the upper Midsouth. The television station had a policy of not selling time for religious programs. Instead, time was provided on a rotation basis to the larger churches. Evangel Temple couldn't compete with First Baptist or First Presbyterian in size, but it did have many entertainers from WSM's Grand Ole Opry, as well as pastor Jimmie Snow, who was an unofficial chaplain to Opry people.

"Give us a format," the management told Jimmie, "and we'll try to find you a half hour of television on Sunday morning."

The result was "Gospel Country," emceed by Jimmie and featuring the biggest names in country music as guest artists. Between numbers and occasional testimonies, Jimmie ad-libbed Scripture and talked up Evangel Temple. The air time was free, but the program still cost the church about $500 a week in union wages to the stagehands and musicians. Within a few months, "Gospel Country" had the second largest Sunday television-viewing audience in Nashville.

In the arrangement with WSM, Opry talent would guest on the program. When making selections, Jimmie didn't check on the performers' church attendance or spirituality. He knew that Opry people ranged from the pious to the impious and that some of the most highly touted "gospel" singers in Nashville were not saints either.

One of the first "Gospel Country" shows featured Connie Smith, one of the fastest rising stars in country music. A hundred-pound package of honey-blonde dynamite on the stage, Constance June Meador was the idol of thousands of young women. What they didn't know was that Connie's heart was breaking.

As a girl in West Virginia, she and her father had listened to the Opry. When barely five, she had told him confidently, "Someday, I'm gonna sing on that Grand Ole Opry."

When her father died, her mother remarried a bulldozer operator with children, increasing the family to sixteen. They moved to Ohio and became active in a church where Connie sang with her brothers and sisters for services. She was a married woman at twenty-two when the Opry's Bill Anderson heard her at a talent contest in Columbus, Ohio. "You're pretty good," he said. "Come to Nashville and I'll get you on the Saturday midnight show at Ernest Tubb's Record Shop."

In Nashville Connie sang before a huge crowd at the after-Opry entertainment. After she stepped down, a round-faced man with thinning hair handed her a note which said: "Stick with it, no matter what. You've got what it takes." The note, signed "Loretta Lynn," had been delivered by Loretta's husband, Mooney. Connie returned home in high spirit.

Bill Anderson brought her back to Nashville for a demonstration record. When Chet Atkins heard it, he signed her for RCA. She cut her first recording, "Once a Day," on July 16, 1964. Released in August, it became the number one country song in the country by November and stayed there for two-and-a-half months. The next year *Billboard* voted her female vocalist of the year.

More hits followed: "Ain't Had No Lovin',"

"The Hurtin's All Over," and "Ribbon of Darkness," among others. The songs told much of the story of her life. Her first marriage had broken up after her husband tried being her road manager for a while. She had two young sons and her second marriage was now floundering. In addition she had been making weekly visits to a psychiatrist before Jimmie Snow invited her to sing on "Gospel Country."

She sang "In the Garden." Near the end of the show Jimmie noticed her sitting on the far side of the studio in tears. After signing off, he walked over.

"May I be of any help?" he asked.

"I don't know why I'm crying."

"Perhaps God is speaking to you."

She told him about her problems, adding, "I've tried to be good enough to go to heaven. I just can't seem to come up to God's standards."

Opening his New Testament, Jimmie read about Jesus' sacrificial death on the cross. "You can never be good enough for God," he said. "None of us can. That's why Jesus died on the cross for our sins. If you'll ask him, he'll forgive you and make you the person God wants you to be."

She continued crying, the tears smudging her makeup.

"Connie, would you like to pray the sinner's prayer and ask Jesus to come into your heart?"

"Oh, yes," she murmured softly.

They prayed while the other performers and the studio audience looked on.

"Do you believe now that God will keep his promises, Connie?"

"Yes. I know he will."

"Praise God. Let's thank him."

Becoming a Christian didn't save her second marriage, but the experience in the studio changed her life. Immediately she became an active member at Evangel Temple. She also participated in David Wilkerson's crusades, sang for Rex Humbard, and gave her testimony and sang at Campus Crusade's Expo '72 in Dallas. Then on tour to the Far East, she gave her testimony before ambassadors, United Nations' representatives, and many other high officials along the way.

At Evangel Temple she found a "real partner in the Lord." In October 1972 she entered into a happy marriage with Marshall Haynes, a telephone installer.

"I found that God still cared for me after two broken marriages," she told the congregation. "Even if I knew there wasn't a heaven, for the peace that God has given me through Jesus Christ, I'd still want to be a Christian."

Connie Smith found her spiritual moorings when Skeeter Davis was still searching for God. Another Cinderella singer, Skeeter had also had her share of heartaches.

Born Mary Frances Penick, the oldest of seven children, Skeeter had grown up in the poverty of Dry Ridge, Kentucky. Her father had a drinking problem and the family survived only by welfare. "Mary Frances flits around like a skeeter," her grandfather had once observed. From then on, "Skeeter" stuck as her permanent nickname.

When she turned two, her beloved grandfather was murdered on Christmas Day. Every Christmas after that, her mother cried over the tragedy.

As a little girl, Skeeter had listened to the Carter Family on the Mexican border station and the Grand Ole Opry over WSM. Like Loretta Lynn, Patsy Cline, Connie Smith, and so many others, she had dreamed of someday singing on the Opry and meeting the stars.

Skeeter sang to anyone who would listen. Relatives and neighbors gave her nickels and dimes. Once she sang to a peddler, who tossed her candy. "I wanted to please people and have them like me more than anything else," Skeeter recalls.

In high school she and her best friend, Betty Jack Davis, sang together as the "Davis Sisters." They got a regular show on WLEX in Lexington, Kentucky, and from there moved to WJR, Detroit. In 1953 when Skeeter was only twenty-one, their RCA recording of "I Forgot More Than You'll Ever Know," climbed to the "Top Ten." They went on a concert tour that summer. In August their car collided with another head on. The crash left Betty Jack dead and Skeeter seriously injured.

It took Skeeter months to recover physically and emotionally, but by 1954 she was back on the show circuit. During the next five years she performed with Hank Snow, Eddie Arnold, and Elvis Presley.

She joined the Opry in 1959 and married Ralph Emery, WSM's most popular deejay. In 1963 she became the first pure country female artist to sell more than a million records of a song; her hit was "End of the World." That year, however, her marriage hit bottom, and she was divorced the following year.

Skeeter never likes to talk about the experience. All she says is that "the courtship was beautiful and the marriage a disaster. We were very incompatible."

The breakup sent her life into another tailspin. Though raised in Sunday school and converted at age eighteen, she, like so many country musicians, had put her career ahead of God. Realizing her mistake, she began asking around for a good church.

Several show business friends assured her she would love Forest Hills Baptist. "The preacher has a heart for country entertainers," they told her.

She found the church but was crying so hard that she sat in the parking lot until everybody came out. The next Sunday she did the same thing.

After a few Sundays, Pastor Bob Daughtery noticed her sitting alone in the lot. As he approached the car, he saw that she was crying and asked, "Are you all right? Is there something I can do to help?"

"Just pray for me," she sobbed.

Finally drying her tears, she went inside.

From then on, she attended three times every week. But it was three years before she gained "any victory" in her heart. "I felt totally lost, sad, depressed, and unloved," she says. "I felt as if nobody loved me, except Pastor Bob and his wife."

Skeeter now admits that the real blockage was in herself. "I wasn't willing to turn over my life 100 percent to the Lord."

The critical time came during a fateful return flight from Hawaii. All day before leaving, she had premonitions that the flight would end as an oil slick in the Pacific. Friends talked her into getting on the plane despite her fears. Forty-five minutes out of Honolulu, the airplane began shaking violently and seemed out of control.

Skeeter remembers praying, "Lord, if you really want me, I'm ready. For a long time I've felt that I've wanted more of you and less of the world. If you'll get us through this, I'm gonna put you first in my life. Not just when it's convenient, but all the time." The shaking stopped, and the pilot circled back to Honolulu and landed. Mechanics checked the plane but found no reason for the mysterious shaking high above the ocean.

Skeeter says she "never took any drugs, never smoked a cigarette, never touched a drop of liquor, but my divorce left its scars. I was a Christian. I knew the Lord was with me. But I didn't feel any love until after I told the Lord he could have all my life."

In the fall of 1973, a caravan of 30 trucks and

300 long-haired Jesus People, forming the "Christ-is-the-Answer Crusade," set up a tent on a downtown lot. Then they spread out in the area to distribute gospel tracts and invite people to services.

On December 8, between Grand Ole Opry shows, Skeeter was in a nearby shopping center and saw police arrest several crusade members on a complaint of harassment. When she went onstage for the evening show at the Opry, she mentioned the incident: "They've arrested fifteen people just for telling people that Jesus loves them. And that really burdened my heart, so I thought I'd sing you all this song." Then she led the audience in a sing-along of "Amazing Grace."

The Opry had an unwritten policy that entertainers were not to use the stage as a platform for personal opinion on controversial religious or political subjects. Most of her fellow performers felt she had been too outspoken. The police complained to the Opry management. After hearing a tape, the management suspended Skeeter from the Opry until further notice.

Joe Johnson, an editor at the Baptist Sunday School Board, had also witnessed the arrests. "I went to the police and said, 'Why are you doing this? You can't arrest prostitutes and pimps, but you're taking these young kids in whose only crime is to hand out gospel tracts.' They said, 'We're sorry about it. We really don't want to do it.'

"Then I called Chief of Police Joe Casey

about it. I said, 'All those people were doing was talking about Jesus. They weren't cursing, drinking, or smoking pot, just talking about Jesus in a calm manner. And your men arrested them. That's the saddest thing I've ever seen.' Chief Casey said, 'Well, I deplore it, but we had to answer a complaint.'"

Nevertheless, two of the sixteen arrested were convicted of trespassing and served ten-day jail sentences. As for Skeeter, she sang with the "Christ-is-the-Answer" group for a few days and invited them to rest at her farm outside Nashville. Then she left for road concerts.

After fifteen months the Opry lifted her suspension and asked her back. Neither Skeeter nor the Opry management wishes to talk about any agreement reached. "Sometimes you can be too righteous," Skeeter admits. "The Lord taught me that my ego wasn't so big. I had been used to traveling first class, staying at the best hotels. When I went off the Opry, my earnings dropped way down. I had to stay in homes and live as an ordinary Christian."

After returning to the Opry, she heard that her grandfather's murderer was out of prison and set out to find him. She located seventy-one-year-old Dilver Webster living just a few miles from where her grandfather had been killed in 1933. The ex-con was now an old man suffering from cancer, but when Skeeter arrived, he recognized her immediately and hugged her joyfully.

"I've been wanting to see you for years," he

said. "My wife and I have all of your record albums."

He drew back, looking off into the distance as if seeing a vision from the past. "You'll never know how much I regret what happened. I've had to live with it for over forty years."

"You've paid your debt, Mr. Webster," Skeeter assured him. "I forgive you and the Lord will forgive you also."

After some more talk, Skeeter left, feeling happy that she had found the old man and lifted his burden.

She still bears the nickname "Skeeter," although onstage she's more like a blond, green-eyed butterfly, flitting in a long gown or blue jeans, her long hair flying. The old gospel quartet song, "I'll Fly Away," is one of her favorites.

To some, Skeeter gives the impression of a gadfly, but when the occasion demands it, she can be decisive and stand for her convictions.

One time after arriving in a town in Illinois, she learned she had been booked into a nightclub. She immediately told the manager, "There's been a mistake. I don't sing where alcohol is sold."

The man got huffy and Skeeter called her agent. "I can't work this place," she said, but he urged her to go ahead "just this once, since you're already there."

"No," Skeeter declared. "I won't sing and have drunks hollering at me."

The manager came back. "We have a contract and you're going to sing. I'm calling you up and you'd better be ready."

He walked to the front and announced Skeeter. She went onstage but refused to sing. "I'm sorry, but there's been a misunderstanding," she said. "Please understand I don't say this with any condemning spirit. I really love people, but I don't entertain in nightclubs. You may not agree with me and that's your privilege, but I wouldn't want to be singing in a club when my Lord returns." Then she walked off.

"We'll sue you for every cent you've got," the manager fumed.

"They crucified my Jesus," Skeeter said and left.

After getting away, she began feeling sorry for herself and started crying. Then she sensed the Lord telling her, *You stood up for me tonight. I'm going to use you as my instrument in winning souls.*

The club didn't sue and her testimony was the talk of the town.

In recent years Skeeter has become a big attraction overseas. At one appearance in Sweden, she sang gospel songs and gave her testimony before 40,000 people. In Africa she made an agreement with promoters to give a country music show if they'd allow her to close with her testimony and an evangelistic appeal. Singing before crowds of up to 25,000, she saw many Africans come to Christ.

"When I was saved at sixteen," Skeeter recalls, "I wanted to go to Africa. A missionary told me, 'If the Lord tells you that, then go. If it's just you, wait.' I'm glad I waited."

Skeeter has not remarried. She lives in suburban Brentwood near some Opry friends. Her house is something of a menagerie with seven dogs, assorted cats, a dove, and an ocelot. "I love them all," she says. "I love everybody."

A friend whom Skeeter loves dearly is Jeannie C. Riley, now her sister in Christ. The story of how the sassy, sarcastic, sexy "Harper Valley P.T.A." girl in miniskirt and white boots came to Christ and changed her show biz image is still being told all over Nashville.

Jeannie Carolyn Stephenson, born the middle of three sisters, lived on a cotton farm in north Texas. As a little girl she rode the back of her mother's cotton sack into the field; when older, she chopped and picked cotton. Sundays she went with her family to the Nazarene church where her Grandfather Moore preached.

"I always thought of him as Moses sent to lead our family out of the wilderness of sin," she says. She went to the altar twice without surrendering her life. "I didn't really understand the plan of salvation."

At age ten she was bed-ridden with rheumatic fever. Her parents put an old radio beside her bed for entertainment. Listening to the Carter Family, Patsy Cline, Hank Snow, Ernest Tubb, and other country music greats, she learned many songs by heart. She really wanted to grow up and marry Elvis Presley. When she realized the impossibility of that, she locked herself in the bathroom and cried.

At Anson High School she was a majorette and voted "Most Popular Girl." At sixteen she made her first stage appearance, singing Marty Robbins' hit, "I Couldn't Keep from Crying." She walked offstage, hoping they'd call her back to sing again. Show business had gotten into her blood. From there it was a short step to performing for a monthly amateur night held in a country schoolhouse.

At eighteen Jeannie married her high school sweetheart, Mickey Riley. A few months later she graduated at the top of her class.

About that time Connie Smith came out with "Once a Day." People told Jeannie, "You belt it out like Connie. You could make it in show business."

Later, she visited Nashville and cut a demo record. A photographer did a photo session of her in the only dress she had to wear, a bridesmaid's gown she had worn to a friend's wedding back home. When the demo didn't work out, she went home discouraged.

Weldon Myrick, a fellow Texan and friend in Nashville, urged her and Mickey to move to Nashville if they really intended to "get in the business."

In the summer of 1966, just like Loretta and Mooney Lynn a few years earlier, they arrived in an old car pulling a U-haul trailer loaded with their family's possessions.

Mickey worked at a service station. Carrying baby Kim, Jeannie walked from office to office along Music Row, telling producers,

"Please listen to my demo." She budgeted fifteen dollars a week for groceries and bought dresses from discount stores on layaway. Every morning she woke up with one thought, *Maybe this is the day*. After two years she was still waiting for the big break.

A songwriter friend, Jerry Chestnut, hired her as a secretary for fifty dollars a week. "I was the worst typist he ever had," Jeannie admits. "He gave me the job out of kindness so I could be close to people on Music Row."

Unknown to Jeannie, producer Shelby Singleton was looking for a fresh voice to record a message song written by Tom T. Hall. When he heard one of Jeannie's demos, he exclaimed, "That's the girl!"

He called Jeannie and offered her a contract, but she hesitated. Plantation was a new and unknown company. Shouldn't she wait for a better opportunity? "Take it," friends encouraged, and she did.

She cut "Harper Valley P.T.A." on July 26, 1968, a hot, humid day in Nashville. At 2:00 A.M. the next morning Ralph Emery aired the song over his all-night radio show on WSM. The switchboard lit up immediately: "Who was that girl?" "Play it again, Ralph!"

Before she'd even left the studio, Jeannie was certain "Harper Valley" would be a hit. She rushed home to phone her mother. "I've just cut the next number one single in the country. It'll sell a million." The next night she called back. "Forget what I said about 'Harper

Valley' selling a million. It'll sell three million!"

Sales of the song about the widow Johnson's socking it to the hypocritical Harper Valley P.T.A. exploded. A week later the record neared the million mark. Jeannie quit her secretarial job and went on the road. In miniskirt and white boots, she played the Flamingo Hotel in Las Vegas, appeared at the Hollywood Palace with Bing Crosby, and hit the biggest show spots in-between. Within six months she had won a stack of awards and was back home for "Jeannie C. Riley Day" with Texas Governor Preston Smith coming to honor her.

A press release described Jeannie as:

a bouncing, bubbling intrigue of mirth with the beguiling charm of a child. She laughs easily, flits around the room like a skitterish butterfly, asks questions with the naiveté of a five-year-old and consistently flips her waist-length, shining brown locks over her shoulder.

She gives the impression of a vivacious child until she steps in front of a microphone. Then with the aplomb of a seasoned pro, she deepens her tones . . . and turns on the sexiest grit heard in ages.

Another release called her:

the sexiest and hottest item to hit the entertainment scene since Peyton Place's first illegitimate birth shattered the television media.

118

Catapulted into a dazzling new life-style with a beautiful home and chauffeured cars, Jeannie became the center of attention at parties. Important people asked her for autographs. Entertainment personalities treated her like an equal. This world was quite different from the one she'd known as a high school girl in Anson, Texas, or as a secretary in Nashville.

Without realizing it, she started changing. "Producers and agents insisted I live that sassy, sex-pot image, rejecting the old values," she recalls. "It was something I fell, or was dragged, into—not something I really felt. I was forced into a role that wasn't me, but a masquerade. I didn't realize it then, but Satan was trying to dominate my life."

Mickey, still working at the service station, became Mr. Jeannie C. Riley. The marriage couldn't stand the strain of Jeannie's success and they were divorced. "This never would have happened," Jeannie says, "if we'd stayed in church and had known the Lord."

Her dizzy whirl lasted almost four years until she entered the hospital in exhaustion. "I wasn't happy. I was miserable, self-critical, and impatient with myself and life in general. I didn't like the person I'd become."

Her sister Helen gave her a copy of *The Living Bible*. Jeannie, never having cared for the Bible, would have preferred a Gothic novel. At Helen's urging, however, she began reading that particular Bible and found it interesting and absorbing.

A friend brought her Pat Boone's book, *A*

New Song. Many of Pat's experiences mirrored her own: a greenhorn falling in with a crowd having standards different from those by which she had been raised. Pat's deliverance and the healing of his and Shirley's marriage impressed her.

She heard about Connie Smith finding God and a new life. One night backstage she talked with Connie, who was wearing a glittering diamond cross around her neck. "That's so beautiful," Jeannie said. Without a word Connie removed the cross and put it around Jeannie's neck. That gesture made a tremendous impact on Jeannie, who began yearning for the same Christian love evident in Connie's life.

Jeannie started attending Forest Hills Baptist Church, which Skeeter Davis and several other performers were then attending. On the road, she hunted up churches to visit.

One Sunday morning in April 1972, she went to Forest Hills in a low mood. She was singing a hymn when a clear thought came: *Jeannie, if you don't turn to God now, you never will.* When Pastor Bob Daughtery closed his sermon with an invitation to accept Christ, she walked forward to share her decision with the congregation. "I'd never really trusted the Lord until then," Jeannie says. "I'd believed about him, but I hadn't put my life totally into his hands. When I did that, everything began to change."

Her self-criticism disappeared; she accepted herself and stopped demanding too much. Her nervousness and her exhaustion were gone.

When impatient and frustrated, she would pray and become calm. Even her dress changed; her "Harper Valley" miniskirt was exchanged for more modest clothes.

She replaced her risqué lyrics with gospel songs and songs of the heart. Her nightclub performances stopped.

Most important of all, she and Mickey began rebuilding their relationship. In 1975 they were remarried with daughter Kim serving as their flower girl.

During performances Jeannie would casually slip in words of testimony. One night she told about her remarriage to Mickey. Afterwards, a big, burly man approached her. Towering over her, he said gently, "Jeannie, would you pray for me and my ex-wife? Things haven't been right since we were divorced. You told about how you had remarried your husband. Would you pray that the same thing might happen to us?"

Jeannie and Mickey now live happily in a beautiful antebellum home called "God's Country" on a 200-acre farm south of Nashville. Mickey's business is doing well. Jeannie's autobiography, *From Harper Valley to the Mountaintop*, was recently published by Chosen Books.

Jeannie jokingly refers to herself as Jeannie C. Riley Riley since remarrying Mickey. She knows who she is and why she is a country music performer. "God wanted me to be a witness for him," she declares. "He gave me all the talents I have."

6

Getting
in Touch
with God

He sits poised on a wooden stool. Holding a flat-top guitar, this big, square-shouldered man with friendly grin and hair turning the color of his silver boots, bends toward the sea of faces ranging in age from very young to very old.

The drums and the cymbals are quiet as Billy Grammer eases his lips up close to the microphone. "Folks, I'd like to do one of the old-timers that's *real* country music. See how you like it." Then lifting his mellow voice, he recalls for the older folks those nostalgic evenings when families would sit around an old battery radio after the work was done and sing. The song is the timeless "I Was Seeing Nellie Home." When he's through, the applause is loud and long until he does another stanza.

"People love the old songs. They're starved to death for the old traditional music," Billy says backstage. "Who would ever think that

'Nellie' would get six encores on the Opry during the last three months?"

One of the world's top guitarists as well as a vocalist, Billy is one of the most-beloved performers on the Opry, his "home" for the past twenty-one years. As a Tennessee fan puts it, "Billy Grammer's as solid as Gibraltar. He stands for something and doesn't move with every change of the wind."

Billy, who has a son and a son-in-law in the ministry, quickly gives the credit to God for everything he means to country music. "If it wasn't for the Lord, I'd still be out there boozing, chasing, and gambling. The people who know me best know who I was and who I am today. They know the change in my life has to come from the Lord."

If Loretta Lynn is "the coal miner's daughter," then Billy Grammer is the "coal miner's son." The oldest of nine brothers and four sisters, he grew up in the coal communities of southern Illinois. His father, who worked in the deep mines for thirty-six years, died at age fifty-six from leukemia and black lung disease.

"We never knew if Dad would be coming home," Billy recalls. "He was in three major explosions where miners were killed. I once asked him after one if he was scared. He said, 'Well, a little bit, son.'

"'Did you run?'

"'No, but I passed some boys that did.'"

Billy continues to reminisce. "We had a forty-acre farm that wouldn't grow anything but kids, persimmon sprouts, sassafras bushes, and a little corn and soybeans. Being the oldest, I had to supervise the other kids in the field. We weren't any different from our neighbors. Everybody worked and helped one another. If somebody's barn burned, the community put up another one. Same with a house. We didn't worry about being poor. We had plenty to eat and a roof to keep rain and snow off us. And the Wabash River to lay a trot line in."

Billy had most of his first eight grades in a one-room school. In the sixth grade the teacher assigned him to help teach the younger children. It was "the first graders in one corner and the second graders in another," Billy recalls.

"We had strict discipline at school and at home. When dad whistled, kids would fall out of trees and head for the house. It was partly out of fear, yes, but we also respected him. When he did whip one of us, we knew he had a reason. He never beat us up."

Billy also respected his father as a violinist and fiddle player. "Dad had two years in the Army school of music. He was a coal miner and farmer. He didn't follow the music business because he didn't want to be around drinkers. I'm sure he could have made a name for himself, had he wanted a music career.

"I was raised hearing and playing all kinds of music from light classics like 'Humoresque' and 'The Blue Danube Waltz' to country favorites, such as 'The Eighth of January' and 'Sally Good'un.' Name them, I can play them. I learned them in the home. Dad played the fiddle and I accompanied him on the guitar. Then as I got older, I played with him at pie suppers and school and church functions."

Billy married his high school sweetheart, Ruth Burzynski, a coal miner's daughter and also one of thirteen children. "The whole country threw their hands up when Ruth and I got married," Billy laughs. "I think they thought we'd have twenty-six kids. We have only three, but those three have seventy-two first cousins!"

After a short stretch in the Army near the end of World War II, Billy found himself among the thousands of unemployed. A friend wrote of a possible opening with music promoter Connie B. Gay, a disc jockey with WARL, Arlington, Virginia. Billy hitchhiked to Arlington, auditioned, and got a job as vocalist and band leader of Gay's "Radio Ranchmen" on WARL. Billy says, "It was like the old saying, 'Yesterday, I couldn't spell *entertainer*. Today I are one.'"

Billy ran into a young soldier moonlighting as a hillbilly comic and musician in Washington, D.C. The fellow wore a red wig, painted spots on his face, and blackened a tooth. His name was Jimmy Dean. Recognizing his talent, Billy introduced Jimmy to Connie B. Gay. By 1954 Jimmy was a television personality with his own network show.

Billy worked with Jimmy, Grandpa Jones, Hawkshaw Hawkins, and other performers in the Washington, D.C. area for three-and-a-half years. Then he made a million-selling gold record, "Gotta Travel On," which propelled him straight to the Grand Ole Opry where he has been ever since.

At sixteen Billy had made a profession of faith and had been baptized in a Baptist church in Illinois. When he and Ruth moved to Nashville, they transferred their membership. However, Billy never attended, preferring the lifestyle he had been following in the music world.

"I cussed, gambled, and drank more booze than you could stack in a room," Billy admits. "I wasn't an alcoholic—yet. I could drink a fifth of vodka on the rocks and still be on my feet. The boys that worked with me wouldn't even know I'd been drinking."

Home for Billy became just a place to unwind between trips and park his silver boots. "Ruth and our three children were awfully patient with me," he admits. "They had to put up with an awful lot."

When Billy and Ruth's first grandchild was born with irreparable birth defects, Billy noticed that his family was sustained by a deep, inner peace which he lacked. During that same time he was going through entrance rites for the Masonic Lodge. One question they asked him was "In whom do you put your trust?"

Billy replied, "In God." Afterwards he realized that he had lied. "I knew I wasn't putting my trust in anybody other than myself," he says. "This bothered me."

In September, Bob Harrington, the self-styled

"Chaplain of Bourbon Street," held a crusade in Nashville. Relatives who were visiting the Grammers asked Billy to go with them to hear Harrington. Billy had planned on going bass fishing that night, but a prop on his motor was broken, so he agreed to go along. Ruth was then quite concerned about their sixteen-year-old son, William Archie. "Make him go with us," she asked her husband.

"That would be the kettle calling the pot black," Billy replied, "but I'll see that he goes." The boy went but sat away from his family in another part of the auditorium.

As the colorful Harrington preached that night, Billy silently mocked him. Then the mocking turned to irritation: *Why is this preacher picking on me when I'm already a church member?* But when the preacher gave the invitation, Billy went forward to surrender his life to Christ. At the front of the auditorium he saw his sixteen-year-old son. Neither had known the other was going to come forward.

Billy's son came to accept Christ. Billy "rededicated" his life and changed radically. He quit drinking and cursing, began reading the Bible and praying regularly, and witnessed to almost everyone he met. Three weeks later he put down his Bible and said, "Ruth, the Lord just brought to my attention that I was not saved before. For the first time in my life I have an awareness of Christ in my life."

The following week Billy got a call from Bob Harrington. "I have a crusade going in Chattanooga and have to be away one night," Harrington said. "Will you be the preacher and give the invitation?"

"I wouldn't know what to do," Billy countered.

"I know you won't, but the Lord will. Just give your testimony and preside. Others will be giving their testimonies too. You won't have to talk long."

Billy went and about a dozen people accepted the Lord that night.

Billy's son (also called Billy) was already active with Campus Crusade for Christ in Overton High School. Crusade workers asked the older Billy to help with a country music program at Campus Crusade headquarters in Arrowhead Springs, California. He went, but there was a mixup and he decided to return home.

A Crusade leader caught up with the country music star, apologized for the confusion, and persuaded him to stay a couple of days for Crusade's Lay Institute. "I'll always be glad I stayed," says Billy. "They taught me how to win people to Christ without strong-arming them."

After leaving Arrowhead Springs, Billy stopped off to see his daughter Dianne and her husband, Alan Mezger. Newly married, they had moved to Oregon. Before leaving their house, Billy witnessed to his daughter and new son-in-law. Alan subsequently enrolled in Dallas Theological Seminary.

For a while Billy wrestled with the idea that God might be calling him to full-time ministry.

"I soon got over that," he says. "I saw that I had a unique opportunity to be a witness in the music business. I realized that every saved person is a minister, though some are set apart as pastors, evangelists, and teachers. God doesn't say, 'Go this place or that place,' as much as he says, 'As you're going, be my witness.'"

Billy tried to talk with a person about Christ one on one. "A guy would come up and ask me, 'What's new?' I'd say, 'Come over here, and I'll tell you what's new with me.' I found that it was best not to witness to someone in front of a crowd of people."

When Billy decided not to perform in night-clubs again, a friend in the music business warned, "You're getting ready to starve to death." Billy replied, "I've inherited the universe, Chief, so let me starve."

"He looked at me as if I'd flipped my lid," Billy recalls.

"I haven't starved. I even had to go on a diet recently to get rid of twenty pounds. I haven't had a big hit in a long time, but my finances have been solid. Booking agents tempted me awhile with nightclub engagements. I didn't go into big details, but just said, 'My convictions have taken me out of them. Thanks for calling me.'"

Billy knows a lot of "lovable boys and girls in the music business who would like to break away from booze and the nightclub and honky-tonk circuit. They're in a rat race. They're trapped. They'd love to get out of it. They don't realize that they won't break out until the Holy Spirit gets to them."

Billy and Ruth are active in Nashville's Concord Baptist Church. Although not ordained, Billy accepts lay preaching engagements. He tells how he fooled himself about being a Christian in the entertainment world for so long, and then he begins to step on other toes: "You're an auto salesman or a welder. Now I'm going to talk about you. I make my living off you who belong to different churches. I challenge you to examine your life.

"Are you saved? I wasn't until September 21, 1969. I didn't realize I was saved until three or four weeks after that. Now what is the problem? What's the yardstick to tell me whether I am saved or not? It's that compassion and that desire to spread the gospel to everybody I meet—there is the real test. That tells me I'm saved. I didn't have that before. How about you? Do you have that desire to tell others about Christ?"

Such hard-nosed, blunt preaching gets results. Many church people have accepted Christ under Billy Grammer's ministry.

Another result of his conversion is a deeper relationship with his wife, Ruth. With their children out of the nest, she frequently accompanies him on road trips.

All of their children are Christians. Donna is married to a Christian layman and lives in Nashville. Dianne and her husband are in Lake Alamanor, California, where he pastors a church. Young Billy, now a student at Dallas

Baptist Theological Seminary, is preparing for full-time ministry.

"The Lord has been good to me and my family," Billy says. "All of us intend to keep on serving him."

Two years after Billy Grammer "saw the light," the same miracle happened to the sultry, dark-haired singing sensation, Wanda Jackson.

Wanda began singing as a child in the bathtub. "Sing, child, so I'll know you're all right," her mother had instructed her. She took her first guitar lessons at six. Her first radio show came at fifteen. She made her first recording, "You Can't Have My Love," while still in high school.

After working with Elvis Presley at the start of his career, she landed a spot with Red Foley on his "Ozark Jubilee." Grammy Award nominations came in 1964 and again in 1971 when she was chosen to sing on the first live Grammy telecast. Her explosive "Right or Wrong" jumped to the top of both pop and country music charts in the United States and became a world-wide hit.

Along the way she married a handsome brown-eyed IBM executive, Wendell Goodman. Wendell resigned from IBM to become her manager. As a result, Wanda headlined in Las Vegas, the London Paladium, and the Paris Olympia. Her "Santa Domingo" was voted number one in six countries. Puerto Rican fans chose her album, "Salute to the Country Music Hall of Fame," as "The Album of the Decade."

Scandinavian fans acclaimed her their most popular female singer.

She seemed to have everything: a strong marriage, two beautiful children, wealth, fame, and more bookings than she could handle. But she was still unhappy and drank to forget the emptiness and misery. Vowing to quit drinking, she'd stop for one day, but be back drinking the next.

She and Wendell reached the point where they cared for people only as ticket purchasers, record buyers, and applause meters. Her mother kept their children, Greg and Gina, and took them to Sunday school and church at South Lindsay Baptist Church in Oklahoma City. Wanda had joined the church at thirteen, the same year she'd gotten a new guitar, which became more important to her than church membership. Wendell, who knew she was a Baptist and a professing Christian, had said those were good reasons for him to avoid religion.

In 1972 Pastor Paul Salyer began checking the church roll to see who was active and came across Wanda's name and the entry of her baptism twenty-one years before. Checking further, he found she was married and that her children were attending Sunday school. He recalled noticing her in church a few times— an attractive, but cold and indifferent, mother.

After asking the church to pray for the Goodman family, he tried to contact Wanda and Wendell. Since they were on the road so much, it was several weeks before he could reach them for an appointment. Wendell finally agreed that he and Wanda would have lunch with the pastor. "The pastor didn't come on strong," Wendell recalls. "He didn't hit us on the head with a Bible and tell us we were heading for hell."

"I talked to them about life," Pastor Salyer says. "They had everything the world could offer, but they didn't appear to be happy. I urged them to try Christ if they wanted to find the real meaning of life."

"Perhaps someone had tried to tell us about Jesus before," Wanda says, "but until that day I'd never known *how* to become a Christian."

However, Wanda and Wendell made no public commitment and left the next day for three weeks of engagements in Alaska. When they returned home, they went to church. As the pastor gave the invitation to trust in Christ, Wanda seemed to hear a voice say, *Walk with me.* Turning to Wendell, she whispered, "Honey, there is something I must do."

"Me, too," he replied and they walked hand in hand to the front.

Their life-style changed. Neither realized by how much until Gina prayed one day at home, "Thank you, Lord, for making Daddy and Mama stop drinking."

Eighty percent of Wanda's work had been in nightclubs. She and Wendell had stopped drinking, but should they give up such a large part of her career? They took the problem to their pastor. "He prayed with us about it," Wanda recalls, "but never told us to quit the clubs. God showed us what we must do."

Wanda sang in church every Sunday they were home. As news of the change in her and Wendell's life spread, invitations began coming from other churches. Three months after their conversion, they left by car for services in the First Baptist Church of Houston, Texas. They stopped for Wanda to keep a previously contracted performance in a nightclub. While singing before 2,000 young people, she decided she would never again use her voice to entice people to a place where alcohol was sold. She and Wendell drove on to Houston where they both dedicated Wanda's career completely to God.

With extra time on their hands, they were able to spend more time with their children. Both Gina and Greg accepted Christ the following year.

When Wanda and Wendell accompanied their pastor to Kentucky for a revival, the crowds were so large that double services had to be scheduled. Many had come just to hear Wanda sing but stayed to accept Christ.

Their faith was tested by Greg's severe asthmatic condition. When all local medical help was exhausted, Pastor Salyer suggested they take the boy to a Christian doctor he knew in Ada, Oklahoma. This doctor recommended some changes in Greg's life-style. In a few months the asthma was relieved to the extent that Greg could even play basketball!

Unlike many stars, Wanda had never recorded religious songs before her conversion. Now she felt free to do her first sacred album. Titled

"Praise the Lord," it was a big success.

"Some people predicted we would starve when we left the nightclub circuit," Wanda says. "We learned to live by Matthew 6:33:

> *But seek ye first the kingdom of God, and his righteousness; and all these things shall be added unto you*

and by Romans 8:28:

> *And we know that all things work together for good to them that love God, to them who are the called according to his purpose."*

Like Billy Grammer, they didn't starve. Performances at rodeos and fairs took up the slack from nightclub engagements. Often after shows, fans would ask Wanda, "Is it really true that you've become a Christian and won't sing in nightclubs?" That kind of question became Wanda's cue to tell them what Jesus had done for her and Wendell.

The two continue to practice their vocations in the country music world. They also give time to revivals and other special efforts to win people to Christ. Everywhere they go, they find opportunities to tell about the new "management" in their lives. "We thought we had everything and we had nothing," Wanda says. "Now we have Christ and find we have everything."

Vocalists, such as Wanda Jackson, Billy Grammer, Roy Acuff, and Loretta Lynn, are the main attractions in country music. Their names go on the marquees and their biographies are featured on the entertainment pages of newspapers. Behind these and other performers are a host of backup musicians, who play in the supporting bands and work as studio musicians in recording sessions. A typical band may include a guitarist, steel guitarist, fiddler, bass player, pianist, drummer, and sometimes a comedian.

These jobs, which demand real artistry, are highly coveted by musicians looking for a secure position with an established performer. Hundreds of pickers and fiddlers come to Nashville every year, make the rounds on Music Row, hang out at restaurants known to be frequented by stars, and wait for the big break. Only the best and the brightest survive.

Bruce Osbon was one. Bruce grew up as a preacher's son in a little town just outside Terre Haute, Indiana. His family listened to the Grand Ole Opry every Saturday night. His Methodist preacher-father played the mandolin, the fiddle, and the guitar. Bruce favored the guitar and made Nashville's Chet Atkins his idol. "I listened to his music day and night and tried to memorize his style," Bruce recalls.

After high school graduation in 1957, Bruce got married. He worked in a piano factory and picked on the side in schools, at Saturday night frolics, and on radio and television. He made two USO overseas tours before getting a job on the "Hayloft Frolic" at an area television station. Still, he wasn't earning enough in music to support a family.

Bruce respected his parents, but by this time he had pretty well broken away from the church. As a child he had gone through the rites of church membership and attended Sunday school, worship services, and Methodist Youth Fellowship. He went until he was too old for his parents to tell him to go. He says, "By the time I was playing professionally, I had pretty much stopped. After working in the factory all week and playing late on Saturday night, I found it easy to sleep in on Sunday morning.

"A true musician is not gonna be happy working at something else," Bruce continues. "Call it laziness or whatever, but he's dedicated to his instrument and he's going to do everything he can to make a living with it. That's the way I was. Everybody I knew told me Nashville was where it was at—the name performers and the big radio, television, and recording studios. So in 1964 I cut out for Nashville."

His wife, Barbara, (not her real name) went along willingly. They rented a drafty old house with a broken roof and ill-fitting windows. Bruce took a low-paying job in a piano store. He tried to make contacts by hanging out at clubs, bars, and restaurants which established musicians were known to frequent; all the time he was hoping to get his face known.

After a few music jobs, he quit the piano store to be available whenever anybody wanted him. Mostly he got calls for road trips, often to substitute for another guitarist who couldn't make the tour. One week he went to Maine with a show troupe in a car. They drove straight through, did one night's engagement, and drove back. The week's work netted Bruce about twenty-five dollars, out of which he had to pay for meals on the road. He didn't complain. Other musicians, hoping to break in, were performing for less.

Sometimes he was on the road for weeks at a time, while Barbara stayed home, trying to keep their two daughters fed and clothed on the few dollars Bruce brought home. At one point they were down to eating canned peaches, which his mother had sent.

Barbara kept begging Bruce to quit the road so he could get a regular job and settle down with the family. But the music business had gotten into his blood and he refused, leaving her only the hope that maybe one day his luck would turn and they would be well off. For himself, Bruce found the road an escape from responsibilities at home.

Bruce says, "I found that people treat you differently on the road. They look up to you. They think you're somebody. You're always onstage with people telling you how great you are. Then you go home and you're just Bruce and Daddy. The toilet's stopped up. She wants you to fix this and that. The money's tight. The kids are crying. Your wife keeps after you. You get no relief until you're back on the road again."

Bruce found alcohol on the road to be as free as tap water. Pills were also easy to come by in Nashville and elsewhere. "There was a doctor in Nashville—he's in prison now—who was the main source for my crowd. I got started from guys who had been to him. I first took pills to stay up and lift my mood. Then I got to love them. One pill, one shot, and I had to have more."

Barbara began warning that she was going to take the children and leave. "Don't go," he begged. "Stick it out a little longer." Finally in 1972 he came home and found his family gone. The house was stripped. She had left only his guitars. "I found out where she was staying, but I didn't ask her to come back," he says.

After the split, Bruce went from bad to worse. In Chicago he overdosed on drugs: "I was lying there hallucinating, thinking I was dying," he recalls. "I felt I was going to fly out the door and hung onto the bed as tight as I could. I kept thinking, *If I can just get to the bathroom and lock my arms around the commode.*

"The doctor said, 'Keep this up and you're going to die sure enough.' But I couldn't stop."

He moved in with a barmaid. When she wanted to get married, he asked Barbara for a divorce. Barbara wanted to wait, hoping they might get back together. "I tried to get you not to leave," Bruce told her. "I never want to go through that again." Barbara reluctantly agreed to the divorce.

Bruce was now no longer able to hold a job. His live-in girl friend was supporting him.

She kept wanting to get married; Bruce kept putting her off.

During this time Bruce never stopped believing in God: "I knew that God was where it's at. I just put him out of my life. Now I was seeing where this had brought me. I suggested to my girl friend that we start going to church. She refused. I knew if I married her, things would be worse. I told God, 'If you'll get me out of this, I'll start going to church.' I didn't say, 'I'll get saved.' At that time, I thought I would be doing God a favor by going to church.

"That same night I caught my girl friend with another guy. I got my stuff and walked out."

Bruce called several Methodist churches in Nashville and found none with Sunday evening services. "I was still too lazy to get out of bed on Sunday morning," he says.

He'd known Jimmie Snow for several years. Jimmie, who had helped him get an occasional job, had also invited him to church a few times. Once he and Barbara had taken the children to Evangel Temple, but "Jimmie's loud preaching scared the kids," Bruce says. "Barbara wouldn't take them back."

Penniless, unfit to hold a job, and desperate, Bruce went back to Evangel Temple: "For a while I just thought I could keep using dope and booze and still go to church. The more I heard Jimmie, the more I realized I would have to be on one side or the other. I couldn't serve two masters.

"I had to be on God's side or the devil's. But

the night I got saved, I wasn't thinking of giving anything up. The desire for alcohol and drugs was gone. I had drugs at the house, but I didn't want them. I was so happy that I didn't think about them. I had guys offer them to me, and I turned them down easy. 'No, thanks. I don't need this anymore,' I said.

"I didn't even know how to pray for a job or anything. I was just happy to be saved and have my sins forgiven. Skeeter Davis called me when she'd heard I'd been saved. She wouldn't have called otherwise. I played for her for five or six months. She did me a lot of good and I love her dearly."

There was never any question about Bruce's talent. When word got around that he was off drugs and alcohol and could hold a job, more jobs became available. After working a few performances for Skeeter, he went on the road with Porter Waggoner. From 1973 until 1976 he traveled with Porter. When Porter quit the road, he became Jim Ed Brown's road guitarist. He continues to help Porter with TV shows and other specials.

He was in Winter Haven, Florida, with Jim Ed's "Nashville on the Road" television show when a preacher friend introduced him to "a sweet Christian girl" named Vickie. They were married the next year and began building a Christian home together.

In 1979 Bruce quit the road: "It was hard to break that life-style. That was all I had known. But it broke up my first marriage and I intend for this one to last."

Bruce continues to do well in the music business. He and Vickie recently bought a new home. As active members of Evangel Temple, they're trying to build a strong Christian marriage. Bruce regularly sees his daughters from his first marriage and is also trying to build a better relationship with them.

If you walk into the living room of his new home, you'll notice prominently displayed pictures of his silver-haired mother and father. "They prayed for me during all the bad years," Bruce says gratefully. "They never quit. One of the first things I did after getting saved was to call them and say, 'Your prayers have been answered. Your boy has found God.'"

7

The Gospel According to Johnny Cash

"Hello, I'm Johnny Cash."

That simple greeting from the big, craggy-faced man with weathered face and brooding eyes is enough to make the audience, any audience, explode in applause.

Country music's legendary "Man in Black" opens another show. Talking or singing in sepulchral tones with a quavering voice aptly described as "sounding like hot gravel dripping from hot molasses," Johnny Cash is the one country entertainer who can perform anywhere successfully.

He's at home in a casino supper club in Atlantic City, before network TV cameras, on a platform with Evangelist Billy Graham, at a maximum security prison, on a stage behind the Iron Curtain (44,000 Czech fans bought out the Winter Sports Hall in Prague a month in advance for one of his concerts), and anywhere else he's called to perform.

The most respected performer in country music, he's also the most enduring superstar musician.

Says the *Wichita Eagle*:

Johnny Cash is an institution. Criticize one of his concerts? Are you kidding!

Observes the *Philadelphia Daily News*:

It doesn't matter how much musical fashions change or how often he appears. Johnny Cash never overstays his welcome. He remains the same.

Johnny has been on five *Country Music* magazine covers—an honor given to no other performer. For his twenty-fifth anniversary in the profession, *Country Music* put out a special edition. The only other musician so lauded is Elvis Presley. As *Country Music* puts it, "Johnny Cash is the longest running superstar."

An obviously wealthy man, he owns song publishing houses in Hendersonville, commands top dollar for appearances, and sells millions of records every year. You can buy Johnny Cash watches, silver patches, tote bags, mugs, and even bells.

"There is no person in the world whom we [Ruth and Billy] have more affection for than Johnny Cash," says Billy Graham. Youth for Christ International named him "Man of the

Year" in 1979 for helping young people. He attends a Pentecostal church outside Nashville, yet he received an honorary doctorate in humanities from Gardner-Webb College, a Southern Baptist school in North Carolina.

Many performers owe their first big break to Johnny Cash.

The Statler Brothers were virtual unknowns when Johnny Cash told them to open his show in Virginia before he had even heard them sing. After they returned home, he called them for another show, then another, and another. With only a handshake they began an eight-year relationship.

Kris Kristofferson says he's "sure I would never have been a performer were it not for Johnny Cash."

Larry Gatlin recalls, "Johnny was one of the first to befriend me when I came to Nashville, the first to take an interest in my old homemade songs. The first to put me on national TV and the first to come bringing gifts to my son, whom we named Joshua Cash Gatlin."

However, no group loves him more than the prisoners for whom he often performs. They know about his brushes with the law and battle with drugs. They know that he is a survivor and a victor, one who understands, one who offers hope. That's why Gary Mark Gilmore, during his last hours before execution at Utah State Prison, called Johnny Cash and asked him to sing "Amazing Grace."

Perhaps "Amazing Grace," written by John

Newton after the hard-drinking, profane, slave trader found God, best describes the journey of Johnny Cash from the pit of despair to the pinnacle of glory. The record shows that he has more lives than ten cats. He wrecked every car he had for seven years, totaled two jeeps and a camper, turned over two tractors and a bulldozer, sank two boats in separate accidents on a lake, jumped from a truck just before it went over a 600-foot cliff in California, brawled and incurred permanent scars, and drove himself into a wild frenzy many times with drugs.

Yet when the raging voices quieted, there was always the "still, small voice" whispering, *I am your God. I love you. I am waiting.*

"The hand of God," Johnny Cash says, "was never off me." In all of his wanderings, Johnny could never escape the "hound of heaven" which pursued him from his childhood.

As a young boy, Johnny had tapped his toes in schoolhouse revivals to the rhythm of guitars, mandolins, and banjos. He'd sung "Shall We Gather at the River?" during baptisms at the "blue hole." He'd been converted at age twelve. "A beautiful peace came over me that night. I felt brand new," he recalls. He felt a touch of heaven when he put his cheek against his dying brother Jack's lips and heard him whisper, "I'm going to a beautiful city. . . . I can hear the angels singing."

Nevertheless, like many other young men

148

from devout homes, he began slipping away from home mooring while in service. He learned to drink while stationed in Germany although he stopped after returning home and marrying Vivian Liberto, a Catholic girl. He didn't argue with Vivian about the requirement of her religion to raise the children Catholic. In fact, he himself usually took them to the Catholic church when he was home.

As a young married man, Johnny got a job as an appliance salesman in Memphis. He spent more time listening to the radio than knocking on doors. Without any professional experience, he applied for a deejay job in Mississippi. The station manager sent him back to Memphis to attend broadcasting school. There he became friends with two music-loving mechanics, Marshall Grant and Luther Perkins.

Their first request to sing came from a Pentecostal church just north of Memphis. "What are we gonna wear?" Luther asked. After thinking about it a minute, Johnny replied, "Why don't we just wear black because black's best for church." It's been black for Johnny Cash ever since.

They sang "Belshazzar," a song Johnny wrote based on a sermon he had heard from the Book of Daniel. Johnny didn't feel comfortable because he hadn't been to church in a while, but he appreciated the loud amens.

He heard that Elvis Presley, the young Assembly-of-God boy from Mississippi, had made a recording for Sam Phillips at Sun Records. Johnny camped outside Sam's office until the manager agreed to hear an audition. "OK, I'm gonna take a chance on you, Cash," he said. "Let's hope you sell."

Johnny recorded a railroad ballad called "Hey, Porter," and a tear-jerker named "Cry, Cry, Cry," which he had written. Sam sent advance copies to deejays, and the voice of young Johnny Cash soon began to be heard on stations across the Midsouth.

Calls for performances started coming. Carl Perkins, a West Tennessean, joined Johnny, Marshall, and Luther. Carl reminded Johnny of his dead brother, Jack, who had wanted to be a preacher. Elvis Presley and a new talent from Louisiana, Jerry Lee Lewis, worked with them. Johnny, Carl, Elvis, and Jerry often harmonized on hymns.

Johnny and his friends left to join the "Louisiana Hayride" on KWKH, Shreveport. He found the atmosphere exhilarating, the crowds noisy and enthusiastic. Backstage, whiskey and beer flowed freely and "snuff queens," available for the night, fluttered among fans asking for autographs. Despite the temptations around him, Johnny walked the line.

He spent his first night away from home after performing in Shreveport. The next morning Johnny, Marshall, and Luther headed for Gladwater, Texas. They kept having to slow down to let cars turn in to churches along the highway. "I ought to go to church," Johnny kept saying.

"Yeah, yeah, I hear you," Marshall agreed. "If you want me to stop somewhere, say the word."

Luther, whose father was a Baptist preacher, said, "I'll go with you."

They never stopped. Johnny didn't realize it at the time, but he was starting a pattern of missing church that kept him from fellowship with other Christians for many years.

When Johnny hit with "Folsom Prison Blues" and "I Walk the Line," his career really took off. From the "Hayride," he moved to the Grand Ole Opry, making guest appearances on national television shows between road tours. By 1958 he had performed in every state in the Union, as well as in Carnegie Hall, the Hollywood Bowl, the London Palladium, and places in Europe and the Far East. About this time he passed another crossroad.

During a long road trip with several Opry artists, one of the performers gave him a little white pill when he became sleepy. Within half an hour he was wide awake and alert. From then on he took amphetamines to stay up. By 1960 he was hooked, nervous, and irritable. On brief trips home, he couldn't sleep and walked the floors, trying to wear the pills off.

Four daughters in quick succession had kept Vivian tied down. As the babies came, she fought against the long trips that kept her husband away from home. She came to hate the career which was robbing her of her husband's companionship.

They moved to California in 1961 with

Johnny vowing to do better. He rededicated his life to Christ and joined the Avenue Community Church in Ventura. He tried to beat the drugs but couldn't. He'd come staggering into the house, mumbling and fussing at Vivian and the girls.

His family came to fear him. Vivian would call his pastor, Floyd Gressett, who would haul Johnny to a ranch hideout and keep him off drugs. Johnny would go back on the road again with good intentions but return hooked. In 1966 Vivian gave up and filed for divorce. Johnny headed back to Nashville.

He began working with the Statler Brothers and the Carter Family. Maybelle and Ezra Carter, loving him like the son they never had, gave him a key to their house. Sometimes he'd lose it, come home crazed from drugs and drink, and kick the door down. June Carter started throwing his pills away. Sometimes he was glad, sometimes angry. She kept saying, "Johnny, I intend to help you, whether you like it or not. God has his eyes on you." But he always knew where to get more.

Stories of the wild and irresponsible antics of Johnny Cash kept the Nashville gossip line humming. Many were true. He had cancelled out on a couple of promoters, leaving them to face bankruptcy. He had painted motel rooms black. He had broken down motel doors, sawed the legs off furniture and beds, tied door knobs together in the night, sounded the fire alarm, and turned baby chickens loose in the corridors.

On one occasion, he and his buddies moved all the beds from their rooms out into the hall, called the room clerk, and then jumped into bed, pretending to be asleep. When the clerk saw them, he called the manager. By the time the manager arrived, the pranksters had reassembled the beds in their rooms and were lying still under the covers. Johnny and a few others developed such a reputation that some motels refused to rent rooms to Nashville musicians.

One night he appeared on the Opry in bad shape. The band had struck up a song, but he couldn't remove the mike from the stand. In a fit of irrational anger he threw down the mike stand, picked it up, and dragged it to the edge of the stage. Then, oblivious to the glass shattering over the stage and into the audience, he began popping the colored floodlights. Afterwards, the Opry manager pulled him aside and said kindly, "We can't use you on the Opry anymore, John."

Johnny responded by jumping into his car and driving recklessly along rain-slick streets through a residential neighborhood. Crying and shaking, he swung around corners on two wheels until the car went out of control and crashed into trees. He totalled the car and climbed out with a broken nose and jaw.

Leaving the Carters, Johnny moved in with Waylon Jennings. He tried hiding his pills from Waylon—to no avail. He decided to buy a house around Old Hickory Lake where Red Foley, Roy Acuff, and several other entertainers lived. Down by a cove, he stopped in front of the oddest residence he had ever seen. The building was at least 200 feet long, with 4 big, 35-foot round rooms, one over the other at each end of the house.

The house was set on a solid rock foundation. Johnny saw in it a symbol of rebuilding his life on the sure Rock of Ages. When the man working at the house said he was building it for himself, Johnny told the contractor Braxton Dixon, "No, this is my house!" Johnny bought the house.

The house didn't help. In October 1967 he was arrested on a drug charge in Lafayette, Georgia, and sent to jail. The next morning Sheriff Ralph Jones had him brought to the office.

Sheriff Jones looked sadly at the star, who was turning into a derelict. "Tell me, Mr. Cash," he said solemnly. "Why would a man like you at the top of his profession let a little thing like this [he held up a pill] destroy his life?"

An uncomfortable silence hung in the room. The lawman dropped his voice. "Mr. Cash, I'm not angry at you, just deeply hurt. I want you to know that my wife and I have followed your career for over ten years. We've bought every record you put out. You probably have no better fans than us. We've always loved you and we're hurt."

Johnny had never felt so miserable and low in all his life.

"Here are your pills. Take them and go. It

will be your decision to destroy yourself or save your life."

"Sheriff," Johnny finally said. "I give you my word that I'll never take another one." Then he walked outside and threw the pills on the ground.

Johnny went back to Nashville and told June Carter about the experience. She made an appointment for Johnny to see Dr. Nat Winston, a psychiatrist and then Tennessee's commissioner of mental health.

Johnny made it through the first night. The next day he found a bottle of amphetamines and swallowed a handful. He got on a tractor and drove it into the lake. As he was crawling out of the ice cold water, his contractor friend, Braxton Dixon, appeared. Close behind came June and Dr. Winston.

June and the psychiatrist took him into the house and put him to bed. "I've seen a good many like you," Nat Winston said seriously. "Many of them didn't make it. There isn't much hope for you unless you get God's help."

June, Maybelle, and Ezra Carter moved into Johnny's house and slept in sleeping bags downstairs to keep the pill pushers away. Another friend sat beside his bed that night. An old drinking buddy managed to get past the first-floor guard and into the room. The "nurse" ran him off with a butcher knife.

Johnny cried and prayed. His days and nights were filled with nightmares. He suffered excruciating cramps and hallucinated. At times he turned wild, leaping about, knocking over furniture, and pulling up carpet. After four weeks of "cold turkey," he believed the battle was won.

In November he and June visited the Baptist church in Hendersonville, a suburb north of Nashville. The pastor, Courtney Wilson, preached on "Jesus, the Living Water."

"I'm going to drink of that living water," Johnny told June. He went out and did his first concert since spending the night in the Georgia jail.

Carl Perkins, who rejoined Johnny that year, had become a slave to alcohol and was trying to fight his own way back to sanity. After a show in San Diego, Carl got drunk again. The next day the group stopped the bus near a beach to have a picnic. Carl, still hung over, began crying that he was dying. June pointed to the miracle in Johnny's life. "Call on God," she urged. "Let him help you, the way he did Johnny."

They got off the bus and left Carl in his bunk. After a while Johnny went to check on Carl and found him standing up, holding a bottle of whiskey with the tears running down his face. "I've quit, John," he declared. "If God could help you quit, he can do it for me."

Carl walked out to the surf and threw the bottle in the ocean. Above the roar of the waves, they could hear him praying, "God have mercy! Help me!" He never took another drink.

After Carl found deliverance, he wrote a

song, "Daddy Sang Bass," about family life as he and Johnny had known it as boys and about the hope of eternity spent in the family circle. The song included a line about Johnny's long-dead brother Jack: "Me and little brother will join right in there"; it became a huge hit.

Johnny had given many concerts in prisons during his bad days. Now with a new song in his heart, he had a message that could truly set prisoners free. In 1968 he went back to Folsom Prison with his old pastor friend, Floyd Gressett, and recorded an album with the Statler Brothers, Marshall, Luther, and June Carter. Johnny's deacon father also went along for the visit. The hardened prisoners were overwhelmed by Johnny's testimony, and a number accepted Christ.

The Carters had become family to Johnny. Sometimes he brought his four girls—Rosanne, Kathleen, Cindy, and Tara—from California to visit Mother Maybelle, Ezra, and June. June had two daughters, Carlene and Rosey, from her failed marriage. The six girls, six to thirteen in age, had a marvelous time together.

Everyone in Nashville seemed to be pulling for June and Johnny to get married. They frequently performed together and were often seen sitting side by side in a church.

Having messed up his first marriage, Johnny was in no hurry this time. Then on a stage in London, Ontario, before 5,000 people, Johnny impulsively said, "Hey, June will you marry me?" June blushed with embarrassment.

"Go on with the show," she urged.

The audience began shouting, "Say, yes! Say, yes!"

"OK," June finally consented. "I'll marry you."

Johnny kissed her and whispered, "I had to ask."

They were wed March 1, 1968, at a church in Franklin, Kentucky. Merle Kilgore, one of Johnny's old music buddies, was best man. Except for Merle's ripping his pocket in getting the ring out for Johnny, the ceremony went smoothly. A nonalcoholic reception, with hundreds of guests attending, was held that night at Johnny's lakeside home. The next morning the newlyweds started their first day together with Bible study.

For some time Johnny's main teacher had been June's father. Ezra Carter had hundreds of Bible commentaries and writings of the church fathers in his home. Johnny couldn't learn enough about the Bible and the growth of the early church.

If the Bible said to make restitution for past wrongs, then Johnny wanted to do it. And if the Bible said help the widows and the orphans, he wanted to do that, too. Johnny Cash had always been known for his generosity. Now his interest in helping others was increased tenfold. Not surprisingly, as word got around about the new Johnny Cash, he was besieged by preachers and representatives of Christian causes.

He and June went to Israel as a follow-up of

their Bible study. Shortly after their return, old friend Luther Perkins died from burns suffered from a fire in his home. Saying good-bye to this faithful friend was very hard for Johnny.

Then there was their good friend, Jan Howard, who had lost a son in Vietnam. They spent a lot of time with her during and after the funeral. When a promoter spoke to them about a tour of American bases in the war zone, they agreed to go. The trip exhausted Johnny, and in Vietnam he caught a terrible cold. There he asked a doctor for pills and also drank some alcohol, the first time since the experience in the Georgia jail. His skin crawled and muscle spasms racked him. Feeling groggy, he stumbled around in a daze. Both he and June knew that he had slipped.

Waiting at the Saigon airport to board a plane for a show in Tokyo, they met Jimmie Snow, who'd come to sing and to preach for the troops. Johnny knew his condition was not hidden from the preacher who had once been on drugs himself. As they exchanged a few words, Jimmie looked him straight in the eye but said nothing about the obvious.

The Tokyo concert was a humiliating exper-ience. Barely able to stand onstage, Johnny staggered through the performance. He closed by apologizing for being in such bad shape and vowed that no audience would ever see him that way again. He and June prayed in their hotel. He flushed his remaining pills down the commode and they flew home.

During 1969 Columbia Records sold 6 million Johnny Cash records, one of every five country records marketed in the United States that year. The Opry took him back. ABC-TV signed him for a series of shows. He set up his own company, the House of Cash, to publish music and market Johnny Cash products. He and June had a son, John Carter Cash.

The television series received good ratings, but Johnny wasn't pleased with some of the guests brought on by the producers. He was also unhappy over pressure to keep quiet about his Christian convictions. When time came for the closing hymn on the next show, he refused to follow the usual script. He said, "I've sung lots of hymns and gospel songs, but this time I want to tell you that I feel what I'm about to sing. I'm a Christian." Shortly afterward he heard that the network was unhappy and intended to drop his show.

Jimmie Snow dropped by to say hello during tapings. Keeping silent about Johnny's relapse in Vietnam, he invited Johnny to "come and knock off a few songs at church in memory of Luther [Perkins]." The Cashes were still going to different churches. Johnny and June went to Evangel Temple, but they still didn't commit themselves to the church in which so many of their friends were involved.

Johnny's sister Reba had helped him set up the family company, the House of Cash. His sister Joanne arrived from Houston and began working for the company. "I was just divorced, drinking, and on drugs," she recalls, "and if it hadn't been for my children, I might have committed suicide. In this condition I called Johnny and he told me to come to Nashville.

"'I love you, little sister, and want you,' he said. I threw my three kids in the car and drove straight through—so stoned with drugs that I couldn't remember the trip afterwards."

Dottie Lee, daughter of old-time country performers Radio Dot and Smokey, was then the receptionist at the House of Cash. She had recently become a Christian at Evangel Temple.

Day after day Dottie witnessed to Joanne, reminding her that Christ could solve her problems. Joanne finally told her, "Dottie, please forget about me. There's no hope. I'm too far gone."

The Cash family had a reunion in Arkansas every October. Johnny rented a plane for flying his family and his sisters over. On the way back they flew into a fierce thunderstorm. As the plane bounced in the black air, Johnny saw that Joanne was white with fright. He made the OK sign with his thumb and finger, but Joanne began screaming, "Jesus, help me! Jesus, help me! Jesus, if you'll save us, I'll go to church with Dottie." Joanne was sure this was her last chance.

The next Sunday as Joanne was entering Evangel Temple, a powerful force seemed to knock her back. She ran, jumped into her car, and drove home.

All that week she felt miserable. On Sunday morning she went back and sat in the second row. When Jimmie Snow gave the invitation for salvation, she was the first one at the altar. She prayed for two hours "not for Jesus to save me," she says, "but for me to accept that he really did love me." Joanne later married Harry Yates, a minister in the church. They now serve in an evangelistic ministry.

Joanne took June's twelve-year-old daughter, Rosey, to church. Rosey became a Christian and started working on the rest of the family.

Late one afternoon Johnny called Jimmie. "Would you like to see my little place of worship?" he asked. Jimmie came over, and they jumped into Johnny's jeep and drove to a little cabin in the woods. It was dark by the time they arrived. "Would you dedicate my little church to the Lord?"

Jimmie prayed and then Johnny asked God for strength and guidance. They talked for a half hour before returning to Johnny's house. Jimmie urged Johnny to get his whole family in one church where they could have regular Christian fellowship and hear the Word of God.

A couple of weeks later the whole Cash family went to Evangel Temple. Johnny saw his sister Joanne in the choir and smiling. The congregation sang "At the Cross" and "Standing on the Promises," familiar, old-time songs which Johnny remembered from his childhood in Arkansas. Larry Gatlin, a newcomer to Nashville from a gospel-singing background, sang "Help Me." Johnny thought it was the best song he had ever heard.

The Cashes returned the next Sunday and heard Jimmie preach on Acts 16:31:

Believe on the Lord Jesus Christ, and thou shalt be saved, and thy house.

Jimmie emphasized that a father should be the spiritual leader of his household. Johnny came down to the altar. "Jimmie," he said, "if my house is going to serve the Lord, I need to lead the way." June and the children followed him.

Evangel Temple, already known as the "Church of Country Music Stars," became an even greater attraction with Johnny and June Cash. On any Sunday, people might hear Connie Smith, Johnny Cash, Billy Walker, Larry Gatlin, and Kris Kristofferson. Kris had also gone to the altar at Evangel Temple and had written a couple of gospel songs afterwards. "Why Me, Lord?" is the gospel classic he wrote after hearing Jimmie Snow preach on God's unconditional love.

Trying to protect the celebrities and keep the services worshipful, church elders posted a sign requesting that visitors neither solicit autographs nor take pictures inside the building. The church also had to turn down requests from persons wanting to sing in front of the congregation because so many wanted to show their music to the stars.

It became impossible to keep people away from Johnny Cash. He and June were there every time the doors opened, and they often went to the altar to pray with seekers. One Sunday a man seated near Johnny followed him to the altar. They were hardly on their knees when the "seeker" whipped out a sheet of music and whispered loudly, "Hey, Johnny, listen to this song I've written. I just know it will be a hit."

Johnny was used to this sort of boldness, but at the altar of his church? "Brother," he said kindly, "this isn't the place. Come to my office tomorrow and my secretary will give you an appointment." He later talked to the writer, but the song didn't catch his fancy.

After joining Evangel Temple, Johnny and June made another visit to Israel. Johnny was gripped with the desire to make a film about Jesus, one which would be true to Scripture and down to earth so that ordinary people could understand why Jesus had come and what he could do for them today. He asked Jimmie Snow to be his literary consultant and in 1971 took about thirty people to Israel for the production. Larry Gatlin sang "Help Me" and another song called "Last Supper," written just for the film. Kris Kristofferson sang "Burden of Freedom," a new song he had written.

When the production was finished, it took over a year to get the movie, *The Gospel Road,* ready for theaters. Johnny appeared personally at the film premieres in major cities. His old pastor friend, Floyd Gressett, now retired from the ministry, took the film to every prison which gave him permission to show it. Then after the initial showings, hundreds of photo stills were made for display to churches around the country. No accurate tally of decisions for Christ was made, but the conversions certainly numbered in the thousands. One missionary reported 50,000 commitments to Christ resulting from film viewings in Africa alone.

At the death of Ezra Carter, his Bible mentor, Johnny and June had inherited a large library of biblical and historical works. They enrolled in Bible correspondence courses and faithfully kept up their lessons at home and on tour. Drawn to the plight of orphans, they built two orphanages near their vacation home in Jamaica. Johnny served as president of the Autistic Foundation for Children in the United States.

When recognized for his concern for children during the International Year of the Child, Johnny said, "We *are* our brother's keeper. The whole future of the human race may depend on whether we reach out a helping hand to the homeless and the poor."

For all his good works and reputation for helping people, Johnny Cash has not been immune from slanderous stories in certain media. A well-known tabloid printed reports of rumors that June Cash had kicked singer Jan Howard out of their performing group after learning she was having an affair with Johnny. The story also suggested Johnny had been high on drugs when taping his latest television special and had had to cancel appearances in two Billy Graham crusades because of drinking.

Johnny told reporter-friends, "I swear I've never used heroin or sniffed cocaine. I'm not on pills and haven't been since I was cured several years ago. And June and I are too much in love to ever think of being separated." He explained that both June's sisters and Jan Howard had left his employment for financial reasons: "I had been spending more on my employees than I was making. I told them their time had come. They went peacefully without screaming or kicking and told me they loved me."

Johnny also flatly denied being spaced out on drugs during any television taping. He said he had to cancel appearances with Billy Graham because he had fallen and hurt his leg. "It's a good thing I'm a Christian," he declared. "If I wasn't, I'd break the jaws of three or four people in this town for getting those stories out."

No such stories have appeared in print about Johnny Cash since.

Johnny Cash is more popular than ever. He recently starred in the moving television drama, "The Pride of Jesse Hallum." He can't possibly fill all the requests for performances. At times, thirty to forty fan buses are on the road leading to his lakeside home. Security guards have to be posted to keep people from leaping over the fence surrounding the house.

Since the fan pressure at Evangel Temple

has become too great, he and June have now been attending a small church on the outskirts of Nashville, off the route of the tour buses. Most of the worshipers are plain, working-class folks, the kind among which Johnny was raised. The pastor, John Colbaugh, does all he can to protect the privacy of his celebrity members. About the man whom *Country Music* magazine calls "an institution in country music," Pastor Colbaugh says, "Johnny represents the finest tradition of human nobility and what can be done by God's grace with shattered dreams and the broken pieces of one's past."

Johnny Cash has no intention of retiring. At seventy-five with silver hair and a face deeply etched with the scars of former years, he'll still be greeting audiences with "Hello, I'm Johnny Cash." And the purposeful stride and familiar husky quaver will always be distinctively his.

8

The Preacher
and the
Gambling Man

Nashville was founded Christmas Day 1779 when James Robertson and his shivering band of pioneers crossed the frozen Cumberland River and began building Fort Nashborough on a bluff. The city, named for a Revolutionary War hero, has a metro population of 600,000. Besides being the country music capital of the world, it can boast of a few other achievements.

The first air-mail delivery was launched there in 1878 when a balloon carried a bag of letters from Nashville to Clarksville, Tennessee. The first public school in the United States was established there in 1885. Nashville is also the home of Andrew Jackson and the place where Teddy Roosevelt said Maxwell House Coffee was "good to the last drop."

Second only to New York City in the number of stocks and bonds sold, Nashville ranks seventeenth among U.S. cities in the number of colleges and universities. Vanderbilt University, recognized worldwide for its scholarship, has a replica of the Greek Parthenon near its campus. Meharry College and Medical School has graduated almost half of the nation's black doctors. Tennessee State University, home of the famous Tigerbelles' women's track team, has sent more athletes to the Olympics than any other school in the world.

Moreover, the city leads the world in religious publishing. Locally based Church of Christ, Southern Baptist, United Methodist, Freewill Baptist, National Baptist, and Seventh-Day Adventist publishing houses blanket the globe with religious literature produced in Nashville. If you pick up an English language Sunday school quarterly, hymn book, or Bible anywhere in the world, chances are it was printed in Nashville. The city is also the home of Thomas Nelson, the world's largest Bible publisher, as well as the world center of gospel music publishing and recording.

Actually, chemicals constitute Nashville's biggest industry, with tourism, insurance, aircraft parts, and truck building running strong. But the city is best known for, and gets its dynamic image from, country music.

The statistical superlatives in recordings alone are staggering. Ninety-five percent of all country music records are made in Nashville. Fifty-two major recording studios in town hold more than 16,000 annual recording sessions. There are 270 music publishers, most of them handling country, to keep up with copyrights and song sheet demands.

The business pulse of the multimillion dollar country music industry is Music Row, an uneven gaggle of modernistic edifices and converted residences, strung along three blocks of Sixteenth and Seventeenth Streets in downtown Nashville, just across Interstate 40. One-sixth acre lots, which sold singly for $7,500 in 1955, now go for $100,000 apiece if you can find them. Within these six blocks are 120 production firms, 80 booking agencies, and the offices of countless performers, songwriters, agents, and publishers.

You will often see a star (in tailored jeans and western shirt—the working garb), climbing into or out of a typically chauffeured Cadillac or Continental, en route to, or from, a recording session. Many sessions run into the early morning hours, and an occasional one will last all night. Between the endless tour buses you may spot a "good ole boy or girl," fresh from Hickory Valley, armed with a guitar and a bag of demo tapes on the way to an office in hopes of sweet-talking his or her way past secretaries. One may be humming Dolly Parton's "Down on Music Row, if you want to be a star, that's where you've got to go. . . ."

At the head of Music Row stands the glittering Country Music Hall of Fame. There the tour buses move in to disgorge their passengers for a look at the thirty-one immortals whose faces and honorary plaques overlook instruments and costumes from other days.

You can also see the original manuscripts of hit songs, folk instruments from Africa and American pioneer days, Elvis Presley's "solid gold" Cadillac, and a star's touring bus complete with automated guide. You can even watch a simulated recording session.

Below the museum is the Country Music Association's Media Center where serious researchers listen to vintage records and comb through manuscripts and clippings from bygone days. There you may find a correspondent from *Time* or *Fortune*, a graduate student working on a doctoral dissertation, or a book writer pushing a deadline for a major publisher.

Stepping outside, you might hear the voice of Conway Twitty on an old prison ballad record—"She killed a man and for the baby's sake I took the blame"—booming from across the intersection where streets split off like the spokes of a wheel. The sound comes from speakers on the front of Twitty's Record Shop where you can also buy novelty car tags announcing *Eat More Possum* and *Jesus Saves*. Close by is the Wax Museum where the stars stand in lifelike poses. Up the block is a makeshift barnyard where anyone can sing or play before a sidewalk crowd and then pass the hat as the old-timers used to do.

Blasting away from a booth nearby is a barker from a tour company: "Come along, folks, and see the homes of the stars. Webb Pierce, Eddie Arnold, Minnie Pearl, Tex Ritter, Hank Williams, Hank Snow, the Reverend

Jimmie Snow. . . . See them all. Hurry, hurry, the air-conditioned bus leaves in five minutes. Get your tickets here. . . . Hurry . . . Hurry."

You can also get tour buses for Printer's Alley (Nashville's Bourbon Street), Tootsie's Orchid Lounge (where many stars hung out in the old days), and the Ryman Auditorium. Others will take you to the Johnny Cash Museum (where Johnny's mother is said to greet visitors at the door), Ernest Tubb's Record Shop, Loretta Lynn's Western Store, Opryland U.S.A., and the new Grand Ole Opry House on Briley Parkway.

At Opryland you can visit Roy Acuff's Museum and see memorabilia gathered from almost half a century of performing. Beside the guitars, fiddles, and old show bills, a corner display case contains the Acuff family Bible opened to Jeremiah 12:9:

Mine heritage is unto me as a speckled bird,

the verse on which Roy's most frequently requested sacred song is based.

Opryland U.S.A. is 241 acres of paradise for country music buffs. Entertainment critics are virtually unanimous in their praise for the bright, bouncy, bubbly music presented by 400 young singers and musicians recruited from Opryland auditions of 7,000 young people each year. From "Opryland's upbeat atmosphere . . . Broadway itself could benefit," observes the *Wall Street Journal.* Opryland has a roller coaster and a few other carnival rides, but it is primarily a musical theme park with shows in theaters scattered around the landscaped grounds.

On a steamy day in August a husband-and-wife team are singing the old songs and cracking earthy humor at Martin's Outdoor Theater before an audience on split-log benches. The crowd claps to the music and roars at the corn: "It's so hot today I saw an ole bird pullin' a worm out of the ground with a potholder!" and "It's so dry that I saw two trees fightin' over a dog."

There's also an imitation of Johnny Cash: "A lot of folks asked me why I wrote that song, 'Ring of Fire.' It was a mistake. I got my Ben Gay mixed up with my Preparation H." Actually Merle Kilgore wrote the song, but nobody is checking history today.

The most popular Opryland musical may be "Country Music U.S.A.," a toe-tapping, hand-clapping trip through the history of country music. The young performers dress and sing like the country-music greats they portray. A staid "Carter Family" harmonizes on "Will the Circle Be Unbroken?"; a young "Hank Williams" in white hat moans "Your Cheatin' Heart"; a lanky "Ernest Tubb," wearing a yellow suit and a red bow tie, sings "Walkin' the Floor over You"; a birdlike "Skeeter Davis" wails "It Wasn't God Who Made Honky-Tonk Angels"; a deep-voiced "Tex Ritter" pleads "Do Not Forsake Me, Oh, My Darling"; and there's much, much more. It's a trip down Memory Lane for people over forty and fifty, a chance

for them to relive their adolescence and courting days with the favorite gospel songs and
ballads of blue-collar and rural America.

On the eastern side of Opryland is the new
Opry House with the largest television studio
in the world. Built with brick walls, rusticated
wood panels, and heavy wood-slab doors, the
acoustics are almost perfect. Pew-type, cush-
ioned, curving benches accommodate family
closeness and seat 4,400 people. The gigantic
stage, 110 feet long and 68 feet deep, holds 50
microphones connected to a mammoth con-
sole. In back are twelve dressing rooms, a
lounge where coffee and lemonade are served,
a post office for the stars, and offices for the
management.

Seven Opry shows run each weekend during
most of the year with Saturday night performances the year round. Almost a million
people drive an average of 1,000 miles round
trip to see a live Opry show every year. The
Opry is the oldest, longest running, and most
successful music show in America.

Though it's generally unrehearsed, some performers run through brief warm-ups in dressing rooms. The management never knows
more than forty-eight hours in advance who
will perform on a given weekend. There is also
no advance promotion of the performers, other
than a listing in the Nashville papers on
Thursday.

Opry members come and go, knowing they
have to appear a minimum of twenty-six weekends each year. One week Minnie Pearl may be

in San Francisco, Stonewall Jackson in Toronto, Skeeter Davis in Stockholm, Marty Robbins in London, and so on. They travel the world, but the Opry is home base. It's the biggest bargain in country music—where else can you see so many stars on a six- or eight-dollar ticket?

Performers take turns hosting a fifteen- or thirty-minute segment of songs and light-hearted patter. Special unannounced guests, such as George Burns, Pat Boone, B. J. Thomas, and other celebrities, often appear on the Opry stage. To sweeten the mixture, young up-and-comers frequently have the opportunity to show their talent before the fans and the Opry establishment.

There's neither a dress standard nor a costume designer to check the performers as they go on. Roy Acuff likes to wear a sport coat, tie, and boots. Hank Snow wouldn't be caught dead without his rhinestones. Stonewall Jackson, under his dark, wide-brimmed feathered hat, looks like a cowboy come to Dodge City on a Saturday night in 1880. Grandpa Jones would be lost without his floppy hat and suspendered jeans: "Everything I have on is new—well, all but these britches. They've stuck to me through thick and thin, and I'm not gonna let 'em down now."

Dolly Parton is a fluff of cotton candy or a voluptuous Daisy Mae in a close-fitting jump-suit. Connie Smith is the epitome of modesty in a long gown. Stu Phillips in a three-piece suit could be right out of IBM. They are a special cast of characters with images suited to their different musical styles and their fans' expectations.

An Opry performance is a sort of organized confusion: One group performs, while other musicians wander around offstage, talking, slapping one another on the back, and sometimes tickling the announcer while he's giving a commercial or announcing a station break at a lectern. Behind this melange of rhinestones, jeans, business suits, gowns, and boots are three rows of pews where backstage guests may sit—close friends and relatives of the performers, visiting press, presidents of fan clubs, and celebrities stopping by to catch a colleague's act.

There is nothing in show business to match the Opry. "If you sat down to design a successful show, you would probably do just the opposite of the way we do," General Manager, Hal Durham, declares. Why? Because the Opry attempts to recreate, on an albeit exaggerated scale, the bygone good times when neighbors gathered in somebody's home or at the crossroads' schoolhouse to enjoy a Saturday night of music and good fellowship.

The Opry, however, is not *pure* nostalgia. The fiddlers, the comedy, the clogging, and the old-time ballads and hymns do help create such an atmosphere. But the electronically amplified instruments, the drums, and the sexually suggestive lyrics warbled by some performers displease some traditionalists, who complain that country music has become too slick, sexy, and commercial. Some fans are also upset when a performer does a honky-tonk, cheating song and then assumes a reverent pose for "Amazing Grace." On the balance, however, a lot of people seem to like the Opry the way it runs, for the fans keep coming.

From the early days the Opry has been broadcast by WSM Radio. The initials stand for "We Shield Millions," the motto of the parent National Life & Accident Insurance Company with $2.8 billion in assets. The Opry is unlikely to fold!

Commercial radio was in its infancy when powerful WSM went on the air at 7:00 P.M. on Monday, October 5, 1925. National Life's Vice-president Edwin Craig made a one-sentence announcement; then Dr. George Stover, pastor of the West End Methodist Church, gave a dedicatory prayer followed by the playing of the national anthem. There was a second religious connection because for a time WSM had to share a frequency with WOAN, Lawrenceburg, Tennessee, operated by Dr. James D. Vaughn, a publisher of gospel music. Vaughn, who had his own quartet and record label, was the leading exponent of gospel music in the South at that time.

The new Nashville station hired announcer George D. Hay away from WLS, Chicago, where he had started the WLS "National Barn Dance." Hay, a former Memphis newspaperman, was given free rein to develop WSM programming. One afternoon, so the story goes, an old, white-bearded man, carrying a black case, dropped by to look over the station. It was Uncle Jimmy Thompson, eighty and blind in one eye. He said that he could "fiddle the taters off a vine" and offered to give a demonstration.

"Well, let's hear it," smiled Hay. With that comment, Uncle Jimmy opened the case, removed a pair of rattlesnake rattles and a piece of red flannel ("keeps old Betsy warm at night"), took out his fiddle, and struck up a tune. When he put down his bow, Hay asked if he knew any more.

"Shucks, I've got a thousand," the old man replied. Convinced Uncle Jimmy was a "find," Hay invited him back the next evening to play before the microphone.

On November 28, 1925, Uncle Jimmy led off with a rousing hoedown. After an hour Hay asked if he wasn't getting tired. "Shucks, no," the old man said. "A man don't get warmed up in an hour. I won an eight-day fiddling contest down at Dallas, and here's my blue ribbon to prove it." By this time telegrams asking for more "old-time music" were being sent to the studio. Within a week or so the station had gotten letters and telegrams from every state in the nation.

Billing himself the "Solemn Ole Judge," though he was only thirty, Hay began building a cast of old-time musicians. He hired Dr. Humphrey Bates (a real country physician) and his group as the first country band to play on WSM. He found Uncle Dave Macon, who played the banjo, driving a freight wagon. Uncle Dave, who knew as many songs as Uncle Jimmy knew fiddle tunes, was even adept at naming performers: Dr. Bates' band became the "Gully Jumpers"; another group became the "Dixie Clodhoppers." Uncle Dave christened a duo of brothers "Sam and Kirk McGee from Sunny Tennessee" and himself the "Dixie Dewdrop."

Sam McGee still performs on the Opry; Kirk died in a farm accident in 1975. Sam tells how they were discovered: "They came down to our farm and said they wanted players outstanding in the field. That's where they found us, out standing in the field."

"Judge" Hay's old-time music didn't please some of Nashville's city fathers, who complained that the country musicians were projecting a bad image of Nashville and asked WSM to take them off. Hay went on air, asking listeners if they wanted the fiddlers, pickers, and singers to continue. Letters and telegrams of support came in by the sackful. The station management decreed that the program would remain.

By the fall of 1927 Hay had rounded up about twenty-five musicians, paying each five dollars to perform on WSM's "Saturday Night Barn Dance." Immediately preceding the show, WSM broadcast "The Music Appreciation Hour," a program of opera, symphonic, and light classical music. One evening Hay announced, "For the past hour we've been listening to music taken largely from Grand

Opera. Now we will present the 'Grand Ole Opry.'" And the "Grand Ole Opry" it has been for over fifty years.

Judge Hay, Uncle Jimmy Thompson, Dr. Humphrey Bates, and Uncle Dave Macon were familiar names in small town, rural America for many years. Listening to them and other Opry performers became a ritual for millions who couldn't afford to go anywhere else on Saturday night during the Great Depression. One of their fans was a boy in Plains, Georgia. Years later when Jimmy Carter became president and stood on the Opry stage, he said, "My biggest dream as a boy was to stand where I'm standing tonight."

With the passing years the old timers began dying off. The first to die was Uncle Jimmy Thompson in 1931. Known to be a heavy drinker, he passed out from imbibing one night and froze to death, according to one story. However, his family claimed he caught pneumonia when his house had caught on fire and he had to run outside in his long johns. Dr. Bates died in 1936, a moment after telling his son, "I'm leaving this world."

Uncle Dave Macon, who called himself a religious man, carried whiskey in his "grip," a little black satchel, right onstage. He and Deford Bailey, a black performer, often traveled and did shows together. If a hotel refused Deford a room, Uncle Dave would say, "He's my valet. He stays with me or I'm leaving." Uncle Dave played at the Opry until three weeks before his death. Today a monument to the Dixie Dewdrop stands along a highway outside Nashville. With a bar of music at the top and a banjo underneath, it has a profile of the familiar face with his gold-toothed smile. The bottom caption is the title of one of Uncle Dave's favorite hymns, "How Beautiful Heaven Must Be."

Hay, the Solemn Ole Judge, frequently had to remind Opry performers to "keep it down to earth, boys." In explaining his philosophy, he said, "We try to keep it [the music] homey.... Many of our geniuses come from simple folk who adhere to the fundamental principles of . . . the Ten Commandments. The Grand Ole Opry expresses these qualities which come to us from these good people." Hay died in 1968.

As the Opry became more popular, people began coming into the corridors of WSM on Saturday night. National Life built an observation studio seating 500 so that fans could watch the performance. When the audience outgrew that, the Opry moved to a theater, later to a tabernacle with a sawdust floor, and then to the War Memorial Auditorium, which seated 3,000. When the War Memorial Auditorium proved to be too small, the world's most popular country show took up weekend residence in the Ryman Auditorium in 1943.

Uncle Dave Macon recalled the new place: "Now this tabernacle whar we play was built by Cap'n Tom Ryman for the preacher Sam Jones. Cap'n Tom had six steamboats on the Cumberland River, and you ought to have seen that wharf lined with horses and mules and wagons hauling freight to them boats and bringing it back. Sam Jones preached the Bible so straight that Cap'n Tom went and poured all his whiskey in the river. And he took them card tables and burned 'em up—clean up. All from hearin' Sam Jones preach and gittin' converted. That was how this song came to be written by Cap'n Tom's darkies:

Cap'n Tom Ryman was a steamboat man,
But Sam Jones sent him to the heavenly land,
Oh, sail away. . . ."

But Uncle Dave told only the bare bones of the true story which is one of the most thrilling dramas in the history of American revivalism. Sam Jones was the greatest evangelist the South ever produced before Billy Graham. Tom Ryman was his prize convert. Jones said for years afterwards, "If Tom gets to heaven before I do and the Lord asks me what I'm doing there, I'll just hunt Tom up, put him on my shoulders, and say, 'Lord, here's my apology for being here.'"

Born of a devout family and educated to be a lawyer, Jones had become a drunkard before age twenty-four. He sobered up briefly when his nineteen-month-old child died and then tried a second time when he lost his law practice. At his dying father's bedside Sam pledged to quit drink forever and turn to Jesus Christ. After the funeral, he heard his grandfather preach. At the end of the sermon, he walked forward to make a profession of faith. A week later, he preached his first sermon.

Jones was already a famed evangelist when he came to Nashville in March 1885 and held a revival at the Tulip Street Methodist Church. So many were turned away that local ministers and laymen promised to erect a large tent if he would return. Some Nashville ministers, however, opposed the colorful revivalist. One prominent divine said he enjoyed a circus but preferred not to attend one where Jones was ringmaster. Another pastor complained about Jones' use of "coarse wit and humor to spice his sermons." A librarian said the evangelist's language bordered on the obscene.

The common people, however, loved the black-eyed, heavy-jawed preacher for the same reason that the society crowd despised him. "I believe in puttin' the fodder down low where the cows can get it," Jones often said. His "earthy" language included:

"I like a fast horse, but may the good Lord deliver me from a fast woman."

"You little, stingy, narrow-hided rascals, a fly could sit on the bridge of your nose and paw you in one eye and kick you in the other. You could look through a keyhole with both eyes and not be cross-eyed either."

"The only thing I have to say against the liquor dealer is that he's just like a louse—he makes his living off the heads of families."

"If some of these old moneymongers get to

heaven, they'll be out before breakfast, digging up the golden streets."

"If you want to find Sam Jones, just scratch under the bottom of a dog. If I'm not there, I have just gone to dinner."

"What the alphabet is to a man of learning, repentance is to a man going to heaven."

When Jones began scalding Nashville in May, the city had an elite uppercrust of businessmen, bankers, and university scholars. There was an undercrust of poor hillbilly types, who grubbed for a living and were exploited by the wealthy who drank and gambled at the best clubs. On Sundays, the elite attended the fashionable churches. Jones went after "moneylenders," the tight-fisted factory owners who paid starvation wages, the slum lords, the saloon keepers, and the big club men.

"If I had a church member who was a member of the Hermitage Club," he said in a tent meeting, "I would have him out of the club or out of the church. Show me a pious man that belongs to it, and I will eat the whole business, brick and all. I believe religion is incompatible with those things." The Hermitage was then the most prestigious club in the city.

Jones proved that sixty-eight of eighty-one liquor dealers in the city were members of churches and listed the guilty ones by denomination. Before he left town, the *Christian Advocate* reported:

Drunkards have renounced their liquor drinking; gamblers have given up their evil occupation; church members convicted of complicity with sin, have broken off from wrong courses; thousands of persons of all ages, sexes, and grades of society have publicly announced their purpose to give up their sins and lead better lives.

Many who came to hear Jones out of hatred or admiration stayed to be converted. His May 1885 meetings averaged almost 10,000 a day, one-sixth of the city's population. In almost every service 250 or more went forward to kneel in the sawdust before a rough altar. Tom Ryman was one.

Ryman, fifty-four, owned a large saloon beside the Cumberland River and operated a string of steamboats up and down the river. He hauled freight, but his big money came from liquor and gambling. Every boat had a bar and gambling tables where prominent Nashvillians could indulge their pleasures far from family and society. Ryman, also a charitable man, gave large sums to churches. He was a pillar in the business community and a leader in Nashville society.

Ryman, upset by reports of Jones' preaching, took a gang of ruffians to the tent to heckle the evangelist. That evening Jones preached on a mother's love and hit Ryman in a soft spot. The old captain was one of the first at the altar, crying for forgiveness.

They said that when Tom Ryman set out to

do something, he never did it halfway. Closing his saloon and bars, he had gallons of expensive whiskey, card tables, and gambling devices dumped in the river. His saloon, renamed "Sam Jones Hall," became a place for religious and temperance meetings. He opened a chapel for prayer meetings on every boat and christened one steamer "The Sam Jones."

Ryman then started raising money to build a tabernacle for future meetings held by Jones. Thanks to Ryman's generous giving, the Union Gospel Tabernacle was ready in 1890 at a cost of around $100,000. The first night about 5,000 came into the building, even though it was meant to hold less than that. Many more congregated outside straining to hear the evangelist.

The greatest revival yet came in 1898. On opening night the tabernacle was again jammed. Within a week 15,000 were trying to get in. Many hundreds were converted. Thousands of men vowed to abstain from liquor and gambling marched down the street in a parade led by Jones and Ryman to signify their resolve.

Besides Sam Jones, the most famous Protestant preachers and evangelists of that day preached in the tabernacle: D.L. Moody, R. A. Torrey, T. DeWitt Talmadge, Fay Mills, Billy Sunday, and Wilbur Chapman. When Ryman died in 1905, Sam Jones held his funeral there and proposed that the tabernacle be named the "Ryman Auditorium." Jones died one year later.

As Protestant denominations became embroiled in bitter debate over social and doctrinal issues, revivalism began to wane. Under trustee ownership, the Ryman became the cultural center of Nashville. The greatest opera companies of the world performed there, as did the most famous symphonies and theater casts. Fritz Kreisler, Enrico Caruso, Helen Keller, Katherine Cornell, the Barrymores, Marian Anderson, Arthur Rubenstein, Paderewski, William Jennings Bryan, and even Blackstone the Magician were some of the famous persons who stood where Jones, Moody, Sunday, and other evangelists had once proclaimed the gospel.

By 1940 Nashville had other auditoriums, and cultural tastes were changing. The famous Ryman was empty most weekends until the Grand Ole Opry moved there in 1943. The next thirty-one years would see the greatest stars of country music perform on the historic stage. Red Foley, Ernest Tubb, Cowboy Copas, Roy Acuff, Hank Williams, Patsy Cline, Hank Snow, Tex Ritter, Connie Smith, Loretta Lynn, Jim Ed Brown, Dolly Parton, the Wilburn Brothers, the Willis Brothers, and Skeeter Davis are among those who made the Ryman the "Mother Church of Country Music."

For fifty years no sermon had been delivered from the Ryman stage, and no invitation to repent and believe had been extended by an evangelist. Then, in the fall of 1972, Jimmie Snow talked with Opry officials about taping a weekly radio program for broadcast over

WSM. The television program, "Gospel Country," had become too expensive to continue paying studio employees and musicians their union wages. Opry manager, Bud Wendell, suggested the radio program be done after the Friday night Opry and asked when the church could start.

Two weeks later at 11:05 P.M., Opry announcer, Tom Brown, closed out the evening's last regular Opry segment and said: "Good evening, ladies and gentlemen, welcome to the first broadcast of 'Grand Ole Gospel Time,' coming to you live from the stage of the Grand Ole Opry House in Nashville, Tennessee. Here as your host is Pastor Jimmie Snow."

Jimmie quickly introduced Johnny Cash, who began singing, "Take Your World and Turn It Around," while the audience cheered and clapped. The Evangel Temple choir sang backup from three big risers, which had previously been used for Johnny's network television show.

After interviewing Johnny about his personal faith, Jimmie gave a seven-minute sermon, "What Think Ye of Christ?"

"Tonight you can have an experience with God," he said as the choir began singing softly in the background. "Like Johnny Cash, if you take him into your heart, life can change for you. . . . I'm not asking you to join a church. I'm asking if you've got the courage to lift your hand and say, 'Pray for me. I need to be saved.'"

About fifty people lifted their hands. After

Jimmie's prayer, choir members stepped into the audience to counsel them.

The following Friday night Connie Smith sang and gave her testimony: "It'll be four years in April since I met Jesus. I was having trouble in my second marriage, but God allowed it to be that way . . . because he reached down and saved my soul." After Jimmie's preaching, forty people made decisions for Christ.

Every Friday night an entertainer was a featured guest. Jimmie was careful to stick close to the Bible, be brief, and avoid any controversy that might embarrass WSM and the Opry management, which was providing the stage and free air time over the powerful station. Hundreds of country music fans wrote thanking the church and the Opry for the program. Many said they had become Christians and were attending a church.

By the time Jimmie Snow had begun preaching after the Friday night Opry in the Ryman, the decision to relocate the Opry had been finalized. The new and larger facilities on Briley Parkway southeast of town would be an improvement over the Ryman's sweltering heat in summer and icebox conditions in winter. The Ryman had become a fire trap beyond repair with limited parking facilities. Since the neighborhood had turned seedy, innocent loitering outside the building after dark had also become risky business. Moving would be a definite giant step up for the Opry, WSM, and National Life.

Few opposed the move itself; however, disposing of the Ryman caused a controversy. Some proposed that it be torn down and the bricks be used for building a chapel in Opryland. Roy Acuff said he would attend church there every Sunday. The idea to preserve the building as a museum was finally accepted as the most practical. In addition, a chunk of the old oak stage would be transplanted to the stage of the new Opry House for sentimental reasons.

The last night of the Opry in the Ryman was set for Friday, March 15, 1974. The premiere performance in the new Opry House would be the following evening with President Richard Nixon as honored guest.

That last Friday evening in the old Ryman was a truly memorable occasion. Such tears hadn't been shed there since Tom Ryman's funeral. The show dragged on until almost midnight before the last song of the Opry had been sung and Jimmie Snow's "Grand Ole Gospel Time" was scheduled to go on.

Hank Snow, Johnny Cash and his daughter Roseanne, and three generations of Carters—June, her daughters, and Mother Maybelle—joined Jimmie and the church choir for the special service. After they all sang "Will the Circle Be Unbroken?" each entertainer said a few words. Bowing to the preachers of the past, Johnny Cash gave a patriotic recitation of "That Ragged Old Flag."

Jimmie began preaching at almost 1:00 A.M., but the building and the aisles were still packed. "It's been a long time since Sam Jones stood here and preached hell fire and brimstone to sinners," he said, "and a long time since Captain Tom Ryman was converted and inspired to build this old tabernacle." Then preaching from 2 Corinthians 5:17:

Therefore if any man be in Christ, he is a new creature: old things are passed away; behold, all things are become new,

he compared the moving of the Opry to the life-changing experience of salvation.

Around twenty minutes later, the choir began singing the hymn, "Just As I Am." Jimmie invited those who wanted to receive salvation to stand. So many people stood up that it was impossible for him or Johnny Cash to count them all. Instead of an altar call, Jimmie asked them to say a sinner's prayer:

Jesus, I am a sinner and cannot save myself. I stand on your promise that you will come into my heart. I give myself to you. I love you, Jesus.

Then as the choir hummed softly, Jimmie told the tired and tearful audience, "I pray that you will be so touched with the hand of God that you'll never forget tonight so long as you live." When it was time to go, he said, "The last words as we leave this blessed old building should be: 'And all the people said, "Amen."'"

And they did. Amens reverberated all around the old gospel hall. As the crowd moved out slowly and solemnly, many were still crying.

An era had ended. A new one had begun, not only for the Opry and country music, but for hundreds of fans as well.

Now the old Ryman is open during the day for a one-dollar entry fee. Nostalgic fans move reverently down the aisles, sit in the well-worn curving pews, take the runways leading to the cubicle dressing rooms backstage, stand where the stars once stood, and have their pictures taken. Behind them is the familiar painting of the old red barn with the big logo, WSM GRAND OLE OPRY.

Plaques and glossy, autographed photos of stars are all around the stage, but the most sentimental decoration is "Saturday Night in Hillbilly Heaven," a long mural with life-size paintings of the departed greats. There in full-stage dress are Patsy Cline, Cowboy Copas, Red Foley, Hank Williams, Judge George D. Hay, Hawkshaw Hawkins, Texas Ruby, Maybelle Carter, and many others. Somewhat awe-struck, the faithful fans file slowly past, while the haunting songs of Patsy Cline, Hank Williams, and other favorites stir within their memories.

9

Ministries and Miracles

In the early seventies the evangelical movement within Nashville's country music community boomed. The change in the lives of such stars as Connie Smith, Billy Walker, Billy Grammer, Johnny Cash, and Skeeter Davis made hot copy for newspapers and fan magazines. Much of the publicity centered around Evangel Temple, the fastest growing church in the Assemblies of God denomination.

Then came the shock which rocked the town and dealt a hard blow to the spiritual awakening. Announced by commentator Paul Harvey, the sad news was: "Ex-country music entertainer and preacher Jimmie Snow and Carol are divorcing."

The divorce was reported all over the United States, Canada, and overseas. Columnists in fan magazines ran wild with speculation.

The Snows were the best-known ministerial couple in country music show business. Both had come from prominent Opry families; both had practically grown up on a stage. Thousands of fans had followed their careers since childhood.

Hadn't Jimmie and Carol been the ideal couple? He preached; she played the organ and directed the choir. They had worked together for six years in evangelism. They'd been to Vietnam twice, performing for troops in battle zones; once, an enemy attack had run them off the platform.

By 1971, however, the marriage had started showing strains during Carol's second pregnancy. But their problems had actually begun earlier. Jimmie himself later admitted that he had been too busy with the church to realize what was happening. He had been going one way, preaching, counseling people—many with marital problems—for hours in the church office, and helping Johnny Cash with the film, *The Gospel Road*. Meanwhile, Carol had been leading another life with her friends.

In August Jimmie told his congregation he and Carol were separated. Hoping to shake up Carol, he filed for divorce later in the month. Carol cross-filed. Since Jimmie felt she should have the custody of the children, he withdrew his suit.

The church was in an uproar. About fifty members joined other churches.

Jimmie met with upset officials of the Assemblies of God. After hearing his story and checking with a few people, they permitted him to continue in his ministerial capacity. They warned him that remarriage, however, would seriously violate church doctrine and jeopardize his standing.

Some of the country music personalities in the church had already left. Jimmie told the others, "I want you to stay, but you could be more embarrassed by further association with me." Only Johnny Cash said he would not be swayed.

When Jimmie and Carol's divorce became final, it made the ninth divorce in the church for that year. Some called the church a divorce mill. Jimmie explained that in the previous six years only four Evangel Temple couples had had marriage breakups. "Any church in town our size will have more than that," he said, but no one seemed to be listening.

Another fifty or so members left.

The months following Jimmie's divorce were the hardest in his Christian life. He often felt like quitting the ministry and going back into show business, the only other trade he knew. However, during this period he felt that he had done the best preaching of his life! By actual count more conversions were registered than in any previous six-month time in the history of Evangel Temple. "I was preaching both to myself and the congregation," he says.

In an attempt to ward off gossip, he had a couple of single men board in his house. This strategy accomplished very little. Every time he was seen talking to a woman anywhere or even counseling one in his study, a new tale seemed to start. The critics kept the phone lines humming. A local newspaperman observed, "Snow stories in Nashville have become as popular as Polish jokes." People speculated about whom he would marry next and when.

"There was someone else I came to fear more than the dirt peddlers," Jimmie later wrote in his autobiography. "Myself. I was a virile thirty-seven-year-old male. Human. Subject to temptation. I was smack in the middle of a music culture where sexual indiscretions were sung about, stimulated, and glorified."

Then about a year after his divorce, he and Dottie Lee, the receptionist at the House of Cash, left Nashville to get married. She had been converted at Evangel Temple, and they had known each other since childhood. Her parents, Radio Dot and Smokey, had sung on the Opry during the forties and fifties. A beautiful blonde, Dottie had already been through two bad marriages, out of which had come four children.

Dottie was well liked, but the new marriage stirred up the church even more. Another exodus took place. Denominational leaders asked Jimmie to turn in his ordination papers. Without them, he could no longer be pastor of an Assembly of God church. Evangel Temple solved this problem by voting to withdraw from the denomination. Jimmie continued as pastor, and Dottie took Carol's place at the organ. But his marital breakup and remarriage had sullied his influence and damaged the church's outreach.

As Jimmie Snow was trying to extricate himself from his problems, a new church with a strong outreach to country music people began springing up in the Brentwood area, south of Nashville, where many performers had purchased expensive homes. After the mid-seventies this new church would become the center of worship and ministry with an evangelical thrust among country music people. By 1980 it would become the largest congregation in Nashville.

Its founder, Billy Ray Moore, is not cast in the same image as Jimmie Snow. Reared in a devout Assembly of God home in Arkansas, Pastor Moore had pastored Assemblies of God churches in Tennessee for eighteen years before starting the work in Brentwood. A big, hearty man, who loves a strenuous game of tennis or touch football, he looks and acts like the beloved small-town pastor you would trust with the family heirlooms. Most of all, he loves people.

He says he hasn't bought a new suit or a pair of shoes for thirty-three years. He often wears a tailor-made western-style blue suit and tan boots. "This suit was given to me by Irby Mandrell, Barbara's father," he reports. "He had a heart attack, lost some weight, and his size changed.

"'Preacher, I believe the Lord would have

me give some suits to you. Would you be embarrassed?' he asked me.

"I said, 'No, Brother!' and he gave me five!"

Pastor Moore trained for the ministry at a small Assemblies of God Bible college in Hot Springs, Arkansas, but never attended seminary. "I was once asked if I was Arminian or Calvinistic," he recalls. "I said, 'I don't know. I studied just enough to pass the grade and share the Word.' I don't take a stand on theology. I just share Jesus in the Word, a chapter in every service. I tell the folks, 'I don't want you to believe this because I'm saying it, but because it's the Word.'"

In 1967 he became pastor of the First Assembly of God Church in Nashville with a comfortable salary and a respected place in his denomination. A few blacks began attending services. Gradually the church was able to adjust to their being part of the fellowship. Then long-haired hippies began showing up. The hair and dress bothered some members, but turning them out would be unjust and inconsistent—after all, the church supported a ministry to youth with drug problems. Later on Pastor Moore set up home Bible studies around the city. These attracted some professionals, including a doctor and a lawyer, who began attending services out of a desire to find the food they felt they weren't getting from their own formal churches.

Old-line Pentecostals were concerned that some of the women visitors wore makeup and pantsuits. The church had survived blacks and hippies, but the newcomers from the Bible studies were seen as a real threat.

"I didn't want to cause any split or contention," Billy Ray Moore says. "My wife and I prayed about it for six months, and we felt the Lord leading us to start a new work."

Only thirty-three attended the first service held in a home on Coral Road in south Nashville. A Presbyterian socialite named Peggy Brown invited the group to use her West Meade mansion. "Nobody's been living there since my husband died," she explained. Within two months over 200 were attending, none from the First Assembly of God.

Someone mentioned that the new church lacked a name. "What shall we call it?" Pastor Moore asked. Someone suggested they name it the "Lord's Chapel," since "it doesn't belong to any person or denomination, but to the Lord. And everyone is welcome."

Billy Moore, wanting to do some things differently for a number of years, now had his chance. He suggested that they no longer take up a collection: "I don't find this ritual in the New Testament, except where Paul said to take care that there be no gatherings [offering] when he came. I do find that when the Jews were rebuilding the Temple in Old Testament times, they put a chest down and had people come and give. So maybe we could do that and never put any pressure on anyone."

He led his new parishioners to adopt a system of government by a self-perpetuating board of elders. He proposed that instead of the traditional invitation or altar call at the end of the service, anyone with a problem or a need could have counseling and prayer with an elder in a separate room at the beginning of the service. "That way nobody will respond to an invitation because I persuaded them," he said.

Billy Moore eliminated announcements, which were infrequent, considering how new the church was. He also declined to follow a formal order of service. "Anyone who feels led by the Spirit to give a special song or testimony may do so," he said. After a half hour of singing and sharing, he would give a Bible exposition on one chapter per service.

While encouraging the people to hold Bible studies and prayer meetings in their homes for neighbors and friends, he chose not to have a formal visitation program. "Let's minister to people where we find them, instead of trying to talk folks into coming to Sunday services," he said.

Without any of the usual fanfare and promotion, the Lord's Chapel grew rapidly. By 1973 the group overflowed the mansion and moved into their own property at the corner of Granny White Pike and Old Hickory Boulevard. With about six acres of land, they had an old house to which they added an auditorium. In 1976 the building caught fire, probably from a heater in the baptistry, and Pastor Moore narrowly escaped being burned to death. The damage was repaired, but a year later an arsonist fired the building, probably with a

Molotov cocktail. One possible motive was to protest attendance of blacks at the church. (The Lord's Chapel has remained the most integrated church in Nashville.)

Building inspectors who joined the arson investigators were appalled to find that over 500 people had been crowding the church services. "You can't have more than 300," they said. The church had the remains bulldozed and built a new auditorium to seat 1,500 with facilities for a Christian elementary and secondary school.

By 1979 they were ready to enlarge again, but metro authorities said sewage facilities were inadequate. Looking for larger property, the church soon found 100 acres on Franklin Road, a major artery. The estate owners sold the property, which was valued at $2,500,000, for $700,000 on easy terms to hold down a huge capital gains tax.

The Lord's Chapel attracted worshipers from all over the metropolitan Nashville area. With the encouragement of Pastor Moore and three associate ministers, groups in four distant areas started independent chapels. The largest is the Hendersonville Chapel with about 700 in attendance. The four daughter churches are independent of corporate connections with the Lord's Chapel.

Billy Ray Moore doesn't keep a head count of the country music worshipers in the congregation. He also never asks a performer to sing. "We don't want anyone to think we're trying to use him. If he wants to minister in song or testimony, he can do so, but he has to take the initiative." Connie Smith takes the initiative and also serves as a counselor; her husband, Marshall Haynes, teaches an adult Sunday school class.

Most worshipers come informally dressed. The service begins with a rousing, hand-clapping song and then moves to a slower, more worshipful hymn. Many sing with their eyes closed. Some lift their hands when singing or praying. There are no hymn books so hymns are sung from memory.

Early in the service, the presiding pastor directs those with needs to the special counseling rooms. Pastor Moore says, "Many come because they know they can have a half hour with a counselor while the rest of us are worshiping in the auditorium."

Besides golden-haired Connie Smith, Donna Stoneman of the famous Stoneman Family also counsels at the Lord's Chapel. She's out of town more often than Connie, who has a husband and five children to care for.

"I go to any church, college, prison, or group that will have me," Donna says. "Whether they're Presbyterian, Baptist, Pentecostal, Catholic, or whatever, it doesn't matter. I just share what the Lord has done for me."

Country music fans remember Donna, the dancing, blonde look-alike of actress Debbie Reynolds, as "the world's best mandolin player." Her feet would move in synchronization with her fingers which plucked away on the mandolin. "Five-foot two, eyes of blue, turned down toes, turned-up nose," laughs Donna.

"That image started out being a part of me; then it got to be all of me, and the real me got lost in the shuffle. . . .

"I always had to be my best whether I wanted to or not—keep smiling and dancing—while inside I was about to die. I hid it from the world. Everything in the world became dark to me. . . . I didn't understand why I was born, why I was living. . . . Just like all the hippies and the young kids trying to find answers in drugs, I couldn't find any meaning in life.

"We weren't number one rich, but we had enough. For somebody from a poor background, it was a lot. We had a big, beautiful house, and I had four closets full of beautiful clothes. I had everything, and yet I had nothing.

"My marriage failure was the last straw. I was estranged from my husband, living for a year in a separate room in the same house. I stayed for the family's sake, for the business, for the sake of people. But every time I went smiling and dancing onstage, I could hardly keep from breaking down.

"For a whole year I contemplated how to kill myself. I didn't have access to pills—never was a pill taker. I didn't have a gun, so I couldn't blow my brains out. The only thing I had was a razor blade. So I would sit on the floor with that blade and think how I might do it.

"I had thought I knew Jesus. I belonged to a

church, a cold, structured church. I had stopped going and they didn't even miss me for three years. Then I got a letter asking, 'Where are you?' I was morally good. I made a vow when I was little that I would never drink alcohol, because I had lived around alcoholics and seen what it did. So I promised Jesus I wouldn't drink. But I had never asked him into my life. So I blamed him, and he wasn't even my God.

"My friend, Cathy Manzer, came over. Cathy had been a nun. She just had a form of religion; later she got salvation. She said, 'Donna, pray.'

"I said, 'I'm not going to pray, I'm not going to church, and don't you mention God to me.'

"One night I started to slash my wrists so I would bleed to death. I wanted to, but flashes of hell came before me. And I cried, 'God, oh, God! Help me!' I threw myself down and said, 'I give you my life.' My mandolin had once been the greatest thing in the world to me. 'I give you my mandolin, my talent,' I said.

"That night I made him my Lord, but he wasn't my Savior yet. I still believed you had to be morally good, and I thought God was lucky to have me. I was clean on the outside, but inside I was filthy. I had bitterness and pride and a judgmental spirit, especially pride. But I was ignorant and didn't see the need of salvation until God showed me myself as a little girl who was obedient, doing housework, helping mother—a little girl who was doing it to get her mother and father's attention—and where I had sinned as a teenager.

"I said, 'Oh, God, if you hadn't died for me on the cross, I would go to hell.' I heard a soft voice ask, *What did you say?* I said, 'I would die and go to hell, if you hadn't died for me.'

"I got back to bed and prayed for quite a while, and I said, 'Lord, thank you so much!' And he spoke to my heart again and said, *How do you feel?* I felt like my soul had eaten mints. You know how you feel so clean when you eat a mint? I had never had that feeling, that assurance before.

"I didn't want to go back to the cold church that hadn't known I was missing for three years. I began visiting churches. Every time, I went away empty.

"Some of the pastors wouldn't talk to me, I think, because they felt a single, divorced woman might cause trouble in the church. I kept searching, believing there was a pastor somewhere who would share with me and help me find healing."

During this time Donna's brother Scott, the fiddling champion, died from respiratory and cardiac arrest after drinking shaving lotion. The attending doctor didn't consider it suicide because records showed he had drunk shaving lotion on other occasions. A close friend told a reporter, "It was known throughout the music industry that Scott was a drinker. This type of death is common among drinkers. A person drinks a lot, lies down, and then strangles with fluid caught in the lungs."

Sorrowing over her brother's death, Donna kept searching. Then Jeannie C. Riley told her about the Lord's Chapel. She went to talk with Pastor Moore.

"When I told him my story, Brother Moore said, 'Praise the Lord. I used to pray, "Lord, I hope I get home in time to watch the Stonemans." Your family was our favorite television show. My wife and I would see you dancing and we would pray, "Lord, use that energy for your glory."'"

Before her conversion, Donna had sung only with her family. Now she could sing about God by herself. At the Lord's Chapel for every service, she drank in the biblical expositions and shared her faith with Jeannie C. Riley, Connie Smith, Skeeter Davis, and other believers.

After a while requests began coming for her to sing and to give her testimony. She began going out, trusting God to provide for her needs. She trained herself to use a puppet for children's programs. Named "Sunny Tennessee," it even played the mandolin. She witnessed to every person she could strike up a conversation with in her travels: "I led seven people to the Lord on a plane one year. One was a preacher who didn't know if he was saved. Before I left him, he prayed, 'Lord, I'm a sinful creature. Save me.' I didn't do it. It was the Lord."

At a Presbyterian church in Virginia, the elders drilled her on doctrine: "They asked me this and that. They wanted to know if I was ordained. I just said, 'I love Jesus.' Finally they agreed that I could have the whole service.

When the meeting was over, the pastor got up and said, 'I was very leery about Donna coming, but she can come back anytime.'"

Donna once had a diamond ring worth $600. She says, "The Lord told me I should give it to his work. Later I was on a trip and a woman came and slipped another diamond on my finger. It fit perfectly. I've found you can't outgive the Lord!"

She doesn't consider herself a faith healer, but she does pray for healings if churches will permit it. She also prays for her own healing when there is a need: "I had this ruptured disc. The doctors said, 'You'll have to be operated on immediately. Otherwise we don't give you much chance of walking out of here.'

"I said, 'Well, Jesus told me he would heal me, but for some reason he's using you.' The day after the operation I got up and walked.

"The nurse said, 'I think I'm going to faint. I expected you'd stay flat on your back for at least six weeks!' The Lord uses doctors and he heals either way."

Donna does not ask any set fee for her ministry: "I accept payment for expenses and whatever love offering they wish to give me. For a long time I was embarrassed to take anything. Every time somebody gave me something, I perspired and shook. Then I went to a home prayer meeting where there were seventeen people. I could tell they were all poor while I was dressed nice. When an old man handed me their love offering of fifty dollars, I tried to give it back. 'Sister Donna, don't you dare do that,' he said. 'These people gave from their hearts and you must accept it!'"

Donna now gives all her time to her itinerant ministry and to service at the Lord's Chapel. When music promoters call, she gently explains that she's found a better "Manager." She tells them and anyone else who inquires: "The life I have now surpasses anything I've ever known. It's better than the time our family won the award for the best vocal group of the year. Nothing has ever been so fulfilling as serving Jesus. God has done more than help my broken heart; he has given me a brand new heart. There's no bitterness now, no hurt. I only want to tell my story to help others who may be bitter and have a heart that is breaking."

Her oldest sister, Grace, sometimes travels with her. Some of her other siblings don't quite know what to make of the change in her life. The brothers and sisters are scattered, but once a year they meet for a weekend family reunion on Sand Mountain in Section, Alabama. Saturday is taken up with country music and singing many of the old songs their parents taught them years ago. Sunday morning Donna leads in a worship service. "I hope that one day we can have a family reunion in heaven with Mother and Daddy," she says. "I can't wait to see them again."

Teddy Wilburn is another Opry personality who has found Christ in recent years and attends the Lord's Chapel. His roots in country music go about as far back as Donna Stoneman's.

The oldest of five children, Teddy started life on a hard-scrabble farm in the Arkansas Ozarks. He had three brothers, Doyle, Lester, and Leslie, and one sister, Geraldine. His father, Benjamin, a disabled World War I veteran, worried that he couldn't support his family by farming and trapping foxes.

In 1937 Teddy's father ordered two guitars, a mandolin, and a ukulele on the installment plan from a Kansas City store and built a practice platform behind the house. Soon neighbors began showing up to watch the kids perform.

The next year he mortgaged the farm and bought an old car. For their first professional performance, he drove the family to Thayer, Missouri. The children (Doyle was seven and Teddy six) pulled their instruments from flour sacks and struck up a song in the courthouse square. Passing the hat, their father collected six dollars and forty cents.

They performed in one-room schools and churches; tickets were sold by their parents for fifteen to twenty cents a show. The kids sang on the radio for the first time in Jonesboro, Arkansas. Then trouble struck: Teddy came down with TB, and their house burned down, forcing them to move into the chicken coop.

When Mr. Wilburn heard that Roy Acuff was judging a talent contest in Birmingham, he packed the family into the car. They arrived in a rainstorm just as the winners were being announced. "We'll go around to the stage door and catch Roy when he's coming out," the father said. When Roy emerged, they started singing in the rain. "We must have been a sad sight," Teddy recalls, "because Roy cried."

Roy must have been impressed because he got them on the Opry. Then after six months they were forced off due to child labor laws. Returning to Arkansas, they continued performing wherever they could draw a crowd. Pop Wilburn had picture cards printed of the family, and the children sold them for a nickel apiece. They moved to Hot Springs, Arkansas, and lived in a shed and one room of a tourist court for a while.

In 1948 the family joined the "Louisiana Hayride" in Shreveport, performing Saturday nights and doing a weekday radio show just ahead of Hank Williams. During their stay of three years, they launched the career of Webb Pierce, a young manager of the shirt department at the local Sears Roebuck store. They also featured a young nine-year-old girl singer named Brenda Lee on their show.

The Wilburn Brothers became a highly successful act. Showcased on "American Bandstand," "Arthur Godfrey," and other national television shows, they recorded one hit after another. The biggest was "Trouble's back in Town," which was voted "Country Record of the Year" in the 1962 *Cash Box* year-end poll.

They also toured the United States, Canada, and Europe.

Later on, brothers Lester and Leslie joined Teddy and Doyle in music-related business ventures; sister Geraldine got married. Their song publishing company multiplied to four companies with the brothers serving as producers, booking agents, and managers for many of the biggest names in the business.

In 1960 they gave a contract to Loretta Lynn, a young singer from Butcher Hollow, Kentucky. Under Teddy and Doyle's guidance Loretta Lynn became a superstar. After ten years of their working with her, she broke away. Their differences are still in litigation.

Loretta talks about their relationship in her book, *Coal Miner's Daughter,* but their involvement in her career isn't mentioned in her smash movie. Teddy says: "We spent ten years of our lives eating, breathing, and sleeping the act of Loretta Lynn. When I read the [movie] script, I saw that it barely touched on us. I asked them to just take us out. But it's an excellent movie."

The break with Loretta hurt Teddy Wilburn deeply: "I just about gave up on humanity. I vowed to never help another living human being as long as I lived. I filled myself up with bitterness, hatred, and distrust. I became a heavy drinker and so paranoid that I didn't trust anyone.

"I remember seeing *The Exorcist* and asking a couple of friends if they thought I was possessed because I was no longer Teddy. I had become someone I didn't like. I totally hated everything I represented."

As a teenager, Teddy had decided he would be married by age twenty-five: "I wanted to be young when my children came along, because I was the youngest in my family and my father seemed old. I came close two or three times but continued a bachelor. After I got out of the Army, I was traveling two-thirds of the time. It wasn't just one-night stands with our appearances; it was motel one-night stands, too. I became distrustful of women. I also couldn't see any possible way of giving to marriage what it deserved when I was on the road so much."

Like other country singers, Teddy knew a lot of hymns and gospel songs. He belonged to a Baptist church and had read the Bible through "a couple or three times" with no spiritual support. Teddy says, "At sixteen I had joined the church with some kids I was running around with. I didn't really know what it was to have a personal relationship with God."

Teddy had never been one to share his problems with people. However, he did respect Skeeter Davis and a few other close friends in the music community. In February 1976 he consented to go with Skeeter to the Lord's Chapel. At the last minute Skeeter said that she had to be in Louisville for a television show and urged him to "please go on anyway for you'll love it."

Teddy ran into May Axton, the mother of a friend in the music business, and asked her to go. She agreed if he would go to Sunday school at her church first. He obliged.

When they arrived at the Lord's Chapel, Billy Ray Moore was inviting people to seek personal counseling. "Will you go with me?" Teddy asked May. Together they talked with an elder about Teddy's troubles: "The elder quoted Scripture—I can't remember what— and prayed, but nothing happened to me until three or four days later," Teddy recalls.

"I became afraid someone was going to kill me. In this frame of mind, I called a doctor friend and asked if I could come by his house. When I got there, my body started shaking uncontrollably. Then God spoke to me and said, *I'm preparing you for death*. I started crying, for I was afraid I would die that night. God said, *Not tonight. I'm preparing you for when you do die*. Scriptures started pouring out of my mouth like I had become a preacher. I kept telling the doctor, 'Listen to what the Bible says' and 'I'm being saved!'

"Something like an electric shock ran through my body from head to toe. It happened twice. I left the doctor at the door of his apartment, holding a *Living Bible*. . . .

"I sang hymns all the way home. The lines made sense to me for the first time in my life. Then doubts started coming. Satan tried to tell me that *he* had given me that experience, not God. I said, 'Hold on there, Satan. You can't tell me you would make me feel that way.' I had experienced the most beautiful feeling that I will ever have this side of heaven. I said, 'Dear God, please show me that that was from you and not from Satan.' And that same beautiful feeling swept through my body for the third time.

"When I got home, I just opened the Bible and started reading. My eyes hit the page at Psalm 60. I don't know where I went from there. I was in and out of bed all night long, asking forgiveness for treating people the way I had. I remember getting up the next morning and telling my mother what had happened. I said, 'Mother, where did all the hate go, and where did all this love come from?'"

Now over four years later, Teddy is better able to discern what happened. He says: "I can identify with Paul and his experience on the road to Damascus. I'm sure some people will not understand what occurred to me, but if you have ever lived in the depths of hell on earth as I did, there is no way of explaining how it is when you have been lifted out of that pit by God's hand.

"God has carried me through a lot since. I've had no financial problems, and I've found that he always provides a way. For a long time I prayed for patience. I don't pray for that so much anymore, for I believe I am now a more patient person.

"I'm still learning to love and trust people, really love and trust others. I still don't open up with fellow Christians as much as I should. I do talk to God a lot, basically because I know he and I are the only two that can do anything about my problems. Before, I always tried to work them out on my own. Now I realize that God is working all things together for my good."

Teddy has retained his boyish face and twinkling blue eyes. He and Doyle still bring cheers from crowds. Busy as ever, they perform on the Opry and do tours around the United States and abroad. Perhaps their most popular rendition is a song narrative called "God Bless America." They started giving it on every show from the time the American hostages were taken in Iran; the brothers are still receiving standing ovations because of it.

Teddy lives with his mother, an arthritic invalid, who requires round-the-clock nursing care. About his father, who died in 1965, Teddy says: "Daddy was a very good man. Very stern and hard, though. He didn't know how to express himself. Love was not expressed in our home. It was taken for granted. I don't know what his relationship with God was when he left."

Teddy wants to believe that his deceased show business friends are also in heaven: "Red Foley was touched by God. No doubt about that. So were Elvis Presley and Hank Williams. They touched so many people, especially Hank with 'I Saw the Light.' Hank had to have spiritual help in putting the words down to that song.

"Samson went his own way and suffered. God still came back to him in the end. That is

217

so beautiful. I like to hope those things happen in our personal lives. Maybe it was that way with Presley, Hank Williams, and my daddy. I think there are mysteries of God that you and I still don't know, things that he keeps to himself.

"We shouldn't be too quick to judge. That's one reason I love the Lord's Chapel. Down there we try to accept and love one another. We should because look how much God loves us!

"I couldn't do that five years ago. I am learning to now because God can turn hatred and mistrust into love."

Because of the rigid denominationalism characterizing Nashville's churches (there isn't even a city-wide ministerial conference), the remarkable growth of the Lord's Chapel and its spin-offs is little known or understood. Many Pentecostals consider the Chapel too "worldly" because women come to the services wearing makeup and pantsuits. Stories about speaking in tongues and exorcism of demons have circulated among area Baptists. Similar criticisms have been voiced of Evangel Temple and the revitalized Belmont Church of Christ, which is located on Music Row and is having a strong outreach to contemporary gospel performers.

Dr. Don Finto, with a Ph.D. from Vanderbilt, became pastor of the Belmont Church of Christ in 1971. A tall, lanky Texan, Finto says, "For many years I read Scripture to prove what I always knew, not for God to teach me. Then I began to see that the body of Christ was much bigger than I had thought and that God was really alive. I also came to realize that I was saved and that I could experience the presence and power of the Holy Spirit.

"Before that, I thought I couldn't be saved before I died unless I had confessed all my sins. I visualized serving God for eighty years and having the bad luck of one unconfessed sin and then going to hell. Finally God got my attention in Romans 4:6 where it says our faith is accredited for righteousness apart from works."

Belmont Church of Christ developed very much like the Lord's Chapel with informal services concluding with an exposition of Scripture by the pastor. It grew rapidly as young, jean-clad worshipers jammed the aisles and the vestibule, making two Sunday morning services necessary.

Many of the best-known contemporary gospel artists, including recording star Amy Grant, attend the church. "We have little input among country music people," Pastor Finto admits. "They have offices in our neighborhood, but they go home to the suburbs. They go to the Lord's Chapel, Evangel Temple, or to churches scattered through town. Culture is probably a factor. People tend to get together with those of like interests."

10

*These
Also Believe*

No country star has ever mounted a stage and
proclaimed disbelief in God, the Ten Commandments, and the Bible. If he started to,
his agent would probably set him straight
fast. Fans expect their idols, even such "out-
laws" as Waylon Jennings and Willie Nelson,
to respect God, motherhood, free enterprise,
and the flag, as well as to have a hymn or a
gospel song ready at the end of their concert.

Such pervasive religiosity makes it difficult
to judge the depth of an entertainer's faith.
Cynics around Nashville say the number of
genuine Christians in country music can be
counted on one finger. They include Minnie
Pearl and Johnny Cash maybe, but as one
preacher puts it sarcastically, the rest turn to
God when their marriages break up, when
they can't whip drug habits, or when they
haven't had hits in ten years. Then there are

dreamy-eyed fans who expect hillbilly heaven will hold anyone who ever picked up a guitar or a fiddle.

Country music entertainers, like everyone else, come from a variety of religious backgrounds and are affiliated with various denominations. In Nashville, the denominations generally divide among Pentecostal types, fundamentalists, mainline evangelicals, and liberal Protestants. The various groups seem to emphasize experience, doctrine, church structure, and social improvement, respectively. These are generalities, of course.

Because of their exposure to a wide spectrum of society, many performers appear to be more tolerant of other beliefs than does the public at large. Having professed faith in Christ as children, they more or less grew up in church. Most of them also have a close relationship with the Grand Ole Opry.

Take Wilma Lee Cooper, whose name is almost synonymous with old-time mountain ballads and gospel songs. When you hear her and her "Clinch Mountain Clan" lifting the rafters with "He Will Set Your Fields on Fire" and "Blessed Jesus, Hold My Hand," you can almost see the folks clapping in her childhood Assembly of God church in West Virginia. Back in 1950 the Library of Music at Harvard University named her and her late husband Stoney's group the "most authentic mountain singing group in America."

The oldest of three Leary girls, she started singing country gospel and the old ballads with her family at home. Neighbors began dropping by, and soon the family had invitations to sing in churches and schools.

Their group included an uncle. When he resumed school teaching, Wilma Lee's father substituted a young fiddler he had heard over the radio—"Fiddlin' Dale" Cooper, who also came from a devout family. Stoney—Cooper's other nickname—and the dark-haired Wilma Lee fell in love and were married in 1941.

When their daughter, Carol Lee, was born the next year, they quit the music business. They didn't think they could be both good parents and performers. Wilma Lee stayed at home, while Stoney delivered soda pop from daylight to dark. Soon tiring of what they were doing, they took a job in Nebraska, singing duets and doing six radio programs a day. Two of their most frequently requested songs were "Wreck on the Highway" and "Don't Make Me Go to Bed and I'll Be Good."

During the next sixteen years they traveled 100,000 miles a year around the country. Carrying their repertoire of mountain songs in a satchel, they performed on some of the nation's most powerful radio stations. During one period they sang on WJJD, Chicago, from four to seven every weekday morning.

Roy Acuff had been trying to get them to the Opry since 1938. They finally became members in 1957. Within two years their records soared up to the "Top Ten."

Settled in Nashville, they faithfully attended an Assembly of God church. The closeness and the fidelity of their marriage relationship was the envy of their colleagues. One was hardly ever seen without the other.

Then after twenty years on the Opry, Stoney suffered a fatal heart attack. Fellow entertainer Vic Willis calls him "one of the finest, most decent persons I've ever met. He was always concerned about other people's problems."

"Stoney," declares Grandpa Jones, "was a very religious man. Everybody liked him. He was quiet, but when he got up before an audience, he always had something to say." Roy Acuff pronounces him "the most humble man I ever met."

"Stoney was a Christian," Wilma Lee says with certainty. "I don't worry about where he is. He would want me to keep on." So she continues on the Opry with her band, the "Clinch Mountain Clan." Sometimes she and her daughter, Carol Lee, do duets.

After her divorce from Jimmie Snow, Carol Lee married a staff musician of the Opry. Carol has her own backup group, "The Carol Lee Singers," which goes onstage for almost every Opry performance. They also serve as recording session musicians for some of the biggest names in the business. Carol and her family also attend the Assembly of God church in Brentwood.

Neither mother nor daughter looks her age. At sixty Wilma Lee retains her girlish looks and a strong voice. She is still partial to the old songs of the heart and faith once sung by her family in the mountains of West Virginia.

Kitty Wells, the first "Queen of Country Music," is a few months older than Wilma Lee and is just as solid in her convictions about God and morality. Like Wilma Lee, she's a country veteran whose career and family life are unsullied.

Kitty's longtime friend Priscilla Inscoe, now a Freewill Baptist missionary in Panama, says, "She was a superstar before anybody knew her name. She is very, very reserved and doesn't like to talk about herself. Her life reveals so much more than she will say."

Loretta Lynn recalls, "When I was a little girl, I imitated Kitty Wells on records. When I came to Nashville, Teddy Wilburn said he thought I sang like her. . . . Kitty is still my idol and always will be. She's good and religious and a real serious Christian."

Kitty, born Muriel Deason, started singing in church. At fourteen she got a guitar. At sixteen she met Johnny Wright and married him two years later. It was Johnny who gave her the stage name, "Kitty Wells."

Kitty started her broadcasting career on WSIX, Nashville, in 1937. During the forties she was one of the brightest performers on the "Louisiana Hayride." In 1952 she came to the Opry. That year "It Wasn't God Who Made Honky-Tonk Angels" made her the first female performer ever to reach number one on the country charts.

In fact, she was the number one female country music artist every year from 1954 to 1965 until Patsy Cline replaced her. The recipient of practically every award given in country music, Kitty was inducted into the Country Music Hall of Fame in 1976.

The first woman to rival male performers, she led the way in challenging the chauvinistic themes of so many country songs about bad women leading good men astray in bars and honky-tonks. Her hit, "It Wasn't God Who Made Honky-Tonk Angels," had been written by a man, J. D. Miller, as an answer to Hank Thompson's "Wild Side of Life." Kitty put this protest song on the charts long before women's lib was ever popularized. Then when Webb Pierce came along with "Back Street Affair," Kitty hit back with "Paying for That Back Street Affair."

Kitty and her husband, Johnny, have worked and traveled together their entire forty-two years of married life. Johnny, who negotiated her first recording contract, still manages her career. He sang with Jack Anglin until 1968 when Jack was killed on the way to Patsy Cline's funeral. After Jack's death, Johnny reorganized Kitty's act as the "Johnny Wright-Kitty Wells Family Show."

They're still on the road about 300 nights a year. Their son Bobby, who was on television's "McHale's Navy," travels with them. They have two other children and seven grandchildren.

Kitty, who doesn't care for the increasing number of country songs that treat sex so explicitly, says, "I don't think the real country people really care much for the shady-type songs. They've always stood with us. We always put on a clean, wholesome show, one that a family can enjoy."

Charlie Walker (no relation to Billy) is a fan and friend of Kitty Wells.

Charlie grew up on a cotton farm run by his father, who was also a lawman in a county east of Dallas. Attending both Baptist and Methodist churches "depending on which one had the best softball team," Charlie says he was converted as a child in church. He started singing in honky-tonks at seventeen and got away from the influence of a good home.

Inducted into the service, he sang country blues songs, which became familiar to thousands of servicemen over the Armed Forces Radio Network. After military duty, he deejayed for fifteen years on the CBS station, KMAC, in San Antonio; he was also named one of the country's top ten disc jockeys. Charlie came to the Opry in 1967.

Husky, a little over 6 feet tall, and weighing 185 pounds, he has the distinction of being the best golfer in country music. Every year he plays in several professional celebrity tournaments, but the one which means the most to him is the Pat Boone Benefit in Chattanooga for Bethel Bible School, a home for the children of prisoners.

Two of Charlie's top hits are "Pick Me up on Your Way Down" and "Please, Don't Squeeze My Charmin." Though he headlines in the biggest supper clubs in Las Vegas, Reno, and elsewhere, he himself doesn't drink or smoke. He says, "We have to live in society. There's alcohol in almost every nice restaurant and grocery stores, too. You just don't have to drink it."

Charlie has turned down several beer commercials: "They were real lucrative, but I won't advertise beer or tobacco. There are some songs I won't sing either."

Charlie and his wife, Virginia (a Mormon), have five children: four stair-step daughters, who cling to him like Christmas ornaments, and a baby boy. An elder in the Mormon church, which he joined after marrying Virginia, Charlie believes there's more to raising children than taking them to Sunday school. Every Monday night at the Walker house is "family home evening." Shutting off the television, he gathers the family together for prayer, Bible study, singing, and a discussion of the most important things in their lives.

He recalls, "When I was a kid, we didn't have television. People sat around, played dominoes, talked, and visited. We had time for one another. It's a lot harder today.

"We've seen a turning away from morality. The sixties were very bad; a lot of young people got into the dope culture. A couple of generations of that and we won't have a country. We're all going to have to go back to the basics of family, integrity, the work ethic, and patriotism."

Charlie believes country music "is about as moral as society in general. To tell the truth, some of the wildest people I've seen are conventioneers whom we entertain. We've got a lot of good Christian people in our business and some others who've strayed from the straight and narrow. You can live for God here the same as if you were selling typewriters."

Sonny James, the handsome, dark-haired "Country Gentleman" from Alabama, agrees with Charlie Walker on many principles. However, Sonny refuses to perform where alcohol is sold. His decision has apparently not affected his career. His income from performances and records is reportedly $500,000 a year. He has also had thirty-one number one hit records.

Starting out as "Little James Loden" on the fiddle with the Loden Family, he was only four when Kate Smith presented him his first musical award. He quickly mastered the guitar, banjo, and several other instruments.

In the early fifties when Johnny Cash asked him for advice on living a Christian life, his song, "Young Love," was a sensation among teenagers. Sonny met his own "young love," Doris, in church; they were married and have been loyal members of the Church of Christ ever since.

Though Sonny's done television skits with Bob Hope and others, he considers himself primarily a country singer, not an actor. He prefers the simple tunes, such as "The Snow Is on the Roses" and "Traces."

His taste in suits has darkened (he once wore only white), but he is still called country music's "Mr. Nice." In contrast to so many other performers, Sonny has never tripped on drugs or gone on an alcoholic binge. Nevertheless, he's always willing to do a prison performance or sing for a drug rehabilitation project.

His manager, Bob Neal, says Sonny can't be budged on his beliefs: "He is very religious and has high principles. He believes a Christian life is one that sets a good example."

Larry Gatlin, about fifteen years younger than Sonny James, is a thirty-two-year-old Texan whose Christianity seems more expressive and more controversial than Sonny's. Some country music fans think Larry's practically the thirteenth apostle; others say he's a cocky egoist and a discredit to the faith he professes.

Regardless of who's right, Larry is one of the fastest rising talents in show business. In 1980 the Academy of Country Music voted him "Top Male Vocalist" and his new record "Straight Ahead" as "Album of the Year." Currently a member of the Opry, he appears on the biggest programs on television.

Cradled in Pentecostalism, Larry cut his teeth on songbooks and the back of pews. His mother entered him at age six in a talent contest. Later he sang with his younger brothers, Steve and Rudy, and his sister, LaDonna, in a family gospel quartet; Mother Gatlin accompanied them on the piano. His father was an oil driller whose work took him all over Texas. The family went along, singing in churches and schools wherever they happened to live. Larry emceed the show. Never at a loss for words, he says, "They used to take up a collection in church to get me to shut up."

Only five-feet, eight-inches tall, Larry quarterbacked in high school and at the University of Houston. "I was the littlest one on my team and always a little cocky," he admits.

After graduating from the university, he took a semester in law school and then headed for Las Vegas, hoping to sing in Elvis Presley's backup group. Opry star Dottie West was so impressed with his ability that she sent him a plane ticket for Nashville. When he arrived in May 1971, she introduced him to Johnny Cash, Kris Kristofferson, and other influentials. Confident of success, Larry told them, "The Lord wants me to write and sing songs. That's why I'm here."

His sister, LaDonna, got married and joined the David Wilkerson evangelistic team. Brothers Steve and Rudy followed Larry to Music City and have remained with him ever since. "They're the finest two human beings I know," Larry says. "One is my right hand; the other's my left."

Larry eventually married and had a child, Kristen, named after his friend Kris Kristofferson. One day while driving, Larry had a bad daydream of what Kristen might grow up to be. As a result, he wrote "Penny Annie," a song about a pretty little girl who grows up to be a drug addict and a prostitute.

Larry typically writes message songs with

heavy religious overtones. "Those Also Love" says that the "beautiful people," aren't the only ones who fall in love. "Help Me," written for Johnny Cash's movie, *The Gospel Road,* is a sinking man's prayer.

One evening Larry and Dottie West went to the Union Mission where Merle Haggard was recording an album titled "Land of Many Churches." After observing the derelicts, Larry wrote and recorded his most controversial song, "Midnight Choir," with his brothers. It's about a group of bums who straggle into the mission for supper and then wander back to the streets to find a bottle of wine. They finally pray that there will "be Mogen David [wine] in heaven," and if there isn't, "who the hell wants to go?"

That song brought the Gatlin brothers a pile of protest mail accusing them of being sacrilegious and of making a sick joke of derelicts. Even though they offered to donate their royalties from the song to rescue missions, the complaints kept coming. They finally sent a letter of apology to radio stations, expressing sorrow if "Midnight Choir" had caused any problems and concluding:

> However, we are not sorry that we released the record. We searched our hearts and did what we thought we had to do. . . . God help the wino . . . . doesn't look like anyone else is going to!

Larry never voices any doubts about his calling, although he insists he's not called to be a Billy Graham. "My calling is to sit on a stool and sing songs that I hope ring true."

He is also quick to criticize churches and religion: "Lots of people are trying to be religious because the thing to do is to see and be seen. I hate to go to church on Easter because all I see are the new hats and outfits."

He told interviewer David Graham, "They should take the robes off the choir and the preacher and quit reading prayers and sermons. So many preachers don't preach out of the Bible but just throw a little in . . . . Faith comes by hearing the Word of God."

He also questions the language of some of the old hymns: "I think we have to speak to people on a different level and go beyond 'Shall We Gather at the River?'"

Evangelical Christians can hardly fault his theology. He expounds on grace as "someone loving you when you have nothing to offer in return. That's God. Religion is man-made." Still, he offends sensitivities by using mild profanity in press interviews.

Nevertheless, on the road he's one of the strictest entertainers in the business. He allows neither narcotics nor alcohol on the bus before, or after, a show. When a musician interviews for a job, he tells him, "If you have to get high to play our music, you're the wrong guy."

For a show he and his brothers lead off with a couple of songs; then he says, "Folks, we've invited you into our living room. We're gonna do the best we can for you. If you'll listen with your ears and eyes and heart and soul, we'll all have a good time." Larry offers a standing money-back guarantee, which no fan has taken him up on yet. He also never hesitates to tell a heckler or a drunk disturbing his performance to leave.

The outlaw image projected by some country singers is commercially motivated, he says. Rhinestones and a fancy western outfit also don't appeal to him or to his brothers. The typical Gatlin garb consists of jeans, open shirts, and maybe vests. Larry makes no apologies for their lack of color and flash: "We don't wear claws or white eye shadow. Women don't throw their panties and room keys on our stage either. We're good guys."

He lives with his wife, Janice, and their children—seven-year-old daughter, Kristen, and three-year-old son, Joshua Cash—in a 150-year-old log house on an 84-acre farm in Antioch, Tennessee, just south of Nashville.

Contrary to the image projected in some newspaper stories, Larry admits he has weaknesses. However, he refuses to bend his convictions: "I owe my children more than seeing their daddy busted on a narcotics charge. At least my kids can say their daddy stood for something."

Besides his family, Larry's greatest joy seems to be in helping people through his songs. One evening after a performance, a fan came up and said, "My wife and daughter were killed a year ago in a car accident. If it hadn't been for your songs, 'Help Me,' 'Lighted through the Darkness,' and 'Mercy River,' I think I would have lost my mind." Larry hugged the man.

"That's where it's at," Larry says. "Having a God-given talent with which to touch and help others is more precious than gold. That's what we're here for."

Barbara Mandrell, Larry Gatlin's female counterpart in many ways, is a five-foot-two, ninety-five pound scrapper. Her two sisters, Louise and Irline, perform with her on the NBC-TV show, "Barbara Mandrell and the Mandrell Sisters."

As a close-knit musical family, they were reared in a Pentecostal church "on hand-clapping, foot-stomping gospel music. The Lord has always been part of my family and my growing up," says Barbara, who is happily married with two children.

She's thirty-two, the same age as Larry, and both her career and his skyrocketed about the same time. A "Snow White" (the title given her by *People* magazine) in her personal life, she parallels Larry both in religious devotion and the raised eyebrows she gets from some of her songs.

Barbara sounded her first note on Christmas Day 1948 in Houston. At five she learned how to play the accordion and quickly mastered the saxophone and the guitar.

"We had a problem trying to get her *not* to practice," says her father, Irby. "We had to make her go outside and play with other kids."

When she did play, she preferred the boys' teams. In high school she was the champion "burn-out" baseball player—a game in which two gloved players see who can slam the hardest ball at each other.

At the age of twelve Barbara was "discovered" by Joe Maphis at a musical instrument trade fair in Chicago where she was demonstrating drums. Maphis took her to Las Vegas for a show. That was the start of her performing career.

After turning thirteen, she sang with her father and became a regular on the "Town Hall Party" television show in Los Angeles. She also toured with Johnny Cash, sang with Red Foley and Patsy Cline, and did several overseas tours.

At fourteen she fell in love with Ken Dudney, the new drummer her father had hired for the family band. She dated six other men (five proposed!) before turning eighteen and marrying ex-drummer Dudney, who had become a Navy pilot.

Happily wed, she quit music and moved with Ken to Washington, D.C. She taught Sunday school at the base chapel and had plans of being simply a wife and a mother. When Ken got orders for overseas, she decided to wait out his duty with her parents, who had moved to Nashville where her father was an executive in a musical instrument company.

One weekend she and her father took in the Opry. Sitting in the audience, she became restless. "I belong up there," she told her father and soon got back in the business.

In 1972 she joined the Opry. Her first recordings—"I've Been Loving You Too Long to Stop Now," "Mama Don't Allow No Music Playing around Here," and "Do Right, Woman, Do Right, Man,"—got plenty of attention. In 1973 she made a hit with "Midnight Oil." Six years later she won the two top awards in country music—from the Country Music Association and the Academy of Country Music, which voted her "Entertainer of the Year."

With the same impish smile she had as a little girl, Barbara now performs on the biggest stages and the highest-rated television variety shows in the nation. Only Dolly Parton and Loretta Lynn, among female country stars, are in her league. With all her fortune and fame, Barbara is still, by music writer Don Rhodes' estimate, "one of the most religious, clean-talking, straight-living, people-loving, kind-acting persons I've ever met."

Her career and her family are intertwined. Her father, Irby, is show manager and travels with Barbara and the "Do-Rites" band (named from her song, "Do Right, Woman, Do Right, Man") in the Stratocruiser bus. Her mother makes all of her costumes. Husband Ken, who once served as the official pilot for the governor of Tennessee, manages the financial end of Barbara's career. He usually stays home with their ten-year-old son, Matthew. Matthew traveled 600,000 miles with her before starting school. Four-year-old daughter Jaime now accompanies Barbara on many trips.

Adamantly against drugs, Barbara also thinks that any woman who lives with a man outside of marriage is "stupid." She calls herself a "pro-American everything." She permits her band members neither drugs nor whiskey before, or after, a show and no women in their motel rooms.

Barbara is also strict about the magazines in her house and will not allow a copy of *Playboy* inside. She, along with Tanya Tucker and Charley McClain, turned down requests for *Playboy* interviews, something which Loretta Lynn and Dolly Parton accepted.

Barbara and Ken have no rules about household chores. "We don't have ego problems because he's not insecure," she says. "His job is just as prestigious as mine, and he loves his work as much as I love mine."

They live in a northern Nashville suburb and have vacation homes in Aspen, Colorado, and by a lakeshore in Alabama. Sisters Irline and Louise are at Barbara's often. Louise is married to songwriter-performer, R. C. Bannon, the son of a Pentecostal minister.

When her schedule permits, Barbara attends the Hendersonville Lord's Chapel. She insists her Christian faith is as strong as ever. "I can't sing gospel songs and not mean it. It has to be a part of me. My belief in God and my Christian life are very real."

Barbara is not happy about press articles suggesting she has traded in her country-girl image for a sexy, flashy one. At least one of her Christian performer friends has talked to her about singing songs which seem to justify immorality. He was specifically concerned about the song, "If Loving You Is Wrong, I Don't Wanta Be Right." "Barbara, that isn't the kind of song that's good for you," he suggested.

Barbara says she has turned down some songs, changed others with distasteful lyrics, and refuses to sing profanity. She does admit that some of her songs do not reflect her personal life. "I've never had anyone take my husband away," she told music critic Alanna Nash. ". . . I can sing a [cheating] song and make it believable . . . because every singer should have enough theatricality to make a song believable. . . . The beauty of country music is that it talks about real people."

Barbara doesn't plan on always being a performer. "When I reach the top and start to go the other way, then I'll be through. I'll know when I reach it," she says.

The country folk songs of George Hamilton IV have created no controversy. The lanky, forty-three-year-old North Carolinian from Winston-Salem says flatly, "Cheatin' and drinkin' songs are not my material. The old honky-tonk, jukebox music has never been something I felt I could sing convincingly."

What George does enjoy singing are old ballads, upbeat love songs, and patriotic music. His first big hit, recorded when he was a freshman at the University of North Carolina, was titled "A Rose and Baby Ruth." It sold over a million copies. Other hits were "Early Morning Rain," "Abilene," "That's What You

Get for Loving Me," and the title of his current album, "Forever Young."

Besides being a Grand Ole Opry favorite, George is probably the most popular American country music entertainer in Europe. Called the "International Ambassador of Country Music," he was the first American country singer to perform behind the Iron Curtain.

Overseas, George has been called a "hillbilly." He grew up in a suburb of Winston-Salem where he and his grandfather listened to the Grand Ole Opry every Saturday night over WSM, Nashville. George became a devoted fan of Ernest Tubb, Roy Acuff, Hank Williams, and other greats.

Saving his money from a paper route, twelve-year-old George persuaded his parents to let him visit Nashville and see the Opry. His mother called ahead to friends and pinned a note to his coat to identify him in case of a mix-up. The trip was the highlight of his early youth.

Later he enrolled as a broadcasting major at the University of North Carolina, where he met songwriter John D. Loudermilk and promoter Orville Campbell, the man who discovered Andy Griffith. With "A Rose and Baby Ruth" they turned the thin Carolinian into a celebrity. He later moved to Washington to be on Jimmy Dean's television show and finished his studies at American University.

On a trip home he married "Tinky," his high school sweetheart. George says it was "the most thrilling experience" of his life. They have two sons and a daughter; the oldest son is named George Hamilton V.

From Washington, George and Tinky moved to Nashville where Chet Atkins recorded him on RCA. George also joined the Grand Ole Opry. In the late sixties he began making overseas tours. In 1971 George, Loretta Lynn, and the Glaser Brothers were named winners of *Billboard*'s first annual international country music awards.

During their years away, George and Tinky were homesick for North Carolina. Because the Opry required members to be available in the Nashville area, going home meant leaving the Opry. However, in 1972 they and their three children moved back to North Carolina anyway.

About a year later George was invited to do a television show for the British Broadcasting Corporation in England. That led to five more shows and a weekly television series in Canada. When in London again, he was asked to give a lecture-concert on country music history at the American embassy there.

Alone with his guitar on a bare stage, he chatted about the origins of country music in the United States. He picked and sang "Greensleeves" and "Barbara Allen" and talked about how Johnny Cash is a direct descendant of the troubadours. He also played some tapes from the Grand Ole Opry.

Representatives of the Soviet and Czech governments heard him and invited him to Moscow and Prague. He became the first American country music entertainer to perform in the socialist bloc of European countries.

A Czech string band greeted him at the Prague airport. They took him to a hall where the director handed over a list of songs they had been rehearsing. Every song on the list, including "The Family Bible," was one of his specials. He did four evening performances before packed houses—a total of 28,000 people.

In Prague, he was asked whether his family had been related in any way to the Czechoslovakian people. He replied by telling about the Moravians in North Carolina, who had come from what is now Czechoslovakia. That information led to a visit with the Moravian bishop in Prague. At a Moravian church service, he sang "Amazing Grace" for a congregation of about thirty who had never heard it. Before leaving the small church, he talked to two young people, who told him that in order to join the church, they had had to fill out papers barring them from college. "It made me ashamed of ever griping about getting up and going to church on Sunday morning," he said later.

He repeated his lecture-concert at the Soviet Institute of Foreign Languages where 250 students, speaking fluent English, heard him. After a while, the woman choir director told him, "We'd like to sing with you."

"I don't know any Russian songs," George said.

"We can sing your songs," she smiled. When they began singing "This Land Is Your Land," the chill bumps rose on George's back.

They sang about someone "in the kitchen with Dinah" and "working on the railroad." Then the choir director said hesitantly, "I know a good song, but you might not like it."

"Go ahead," George grinned, and the choir sang, "We're going to lay down our atom bombs, down by the riverside." Again he was deeply touched.

When the time was up, the woman choir director thanked him. "This was so beautiful," she said. "The songs came from your heart and from our hearts."

In 1976 George rejoined the Opry. By then the rules had changed, permitting him to commute to Nashville from Winston-Salem. In the years since, his popularity both at home and overseas has continued to increase. He has also not changed his stance on questionable lyrics.

He considers his newly released album, "Forever Young," (also the title of a Bob Dylan song) the best he has ever done. "I can identify with Dylan's spiritual statement."

George and Tinky are active in their church in Winston-Salem. Performing for Christian groups as much as possible, he says, "There is a better chance today for a religious revival than there has ever been. Youth are searching for what is real."

If George Hamilton IV dampens the hillbilly stereotype of country singers, then Stu Phillips shatters it. Stu is a cultured, college-educated Canadian from Montreal by way of Edmonton and Calgary. He is both a member of the Grand Ole Opry and a recently ordained Episcopal priest.

Dressed in a tailored suit and open white shirt (or sometimes in full tux), he stands just behind the colored lights on the edge of the stage. With the microphone held close to his lips, he sings a number from his newest album: "Born to be a man . . . Born to really live . . . To have a wife . . . To spend my life . . . A daddy born to give. . . ." Then he does another about there being "more to life than drinking beer out of a can . . . more than getting high. . . ." The fans love his soft baritone on soul-lifting songs, which praise marital and familial love.

Stu says: "My new album, 'Born to Be a Man,' pretty much sounds the philosophical tone of my life. I like songs that express in a wholesome way the aspirations of the human heart. That's what country music is. That's why people relate to it so well. It's just the expression of the human heart."

To see Stu Phillips on Sunday morning, take Franklin Road south from Nashville and go on past expansive green lawns. Nearing plush Brentwood, you see the Church of the Advent silhouetted against a wooded hill, its slender cross rising into the cloud-flecked sky.

Except for his white clerical collar, surplice, and robes, Stu looks as he does on the Opry. He speaks softly and conversationally, looking directly at his audience with the typical twinkle and smile. You almost expect him to break into a ballad as he begins his sermon:

"Last Sunday I was resting in the guest room of a home and happened to see four parachutes drifting down. A few minutes later I saw four more, then another four.

"We talked about that during dinner time and about courage and confidence. My host said, 'You probably understand that skydiving is based more on faith than courage.'

"*Faith* is an important word in skydiving and in all of life. I heard of a skydiver who was told, 'Just pull the ripcord. Don't worry about a thing. When you hit the ground there'll be a truck to pick you up.' Well, the young man jumped, counted to ten, pulled the cord, and nothing happened. He looked back at the plane and shook his fist. 'They probably forgot to send the truck, too,' he yelled.

"My friend Mel Tillis said he would have a problem as a skydiver, counting 'wo-wo-wo-one . . . ta-ta-ta-two.'"

Stu describes faith as "falling free into the arms of God's love. Does God ask us to take a leap without anything to go on, with no assurance of promises fulfilled? No foundation? Certainly not!"

Having drawn his audience into the heart of his message, he begins expounding the story of God's calling Abraham to offer his son Isaac as a sacrifice: "Abraham responded to God in total obedience. He didn't question God. He obeyed. Our duty is to believe and trust God, to love and obey him, to bring others to know him, to put nothing in his place, to show him respect in song, word, and deed, to set aside regular times for study, worship, and prayer."

Stu says we have a duty and a responsibility "to work; to pray for peace; to bear no malice, prejudice, or hate in our hearts; to be kind to all God's creatures; to use all our bodily desires as God intends; to be honest and fair in our dealings; to seek justice and freedom for all people; and to use our talents and possessions in God's service.

"That's quite a list. We can't do it by ourselves. We need the outside help that comes through Christ's vicarious atonement. The essence of Abraham's faith is imparted to all through Christ. . . .

"This brings us to making a commitment, jumping out of the airplane, becoming an active participant. . . .

"The abundant life, the promise of the Lord, this is ours the moment we receive Christ. Jesus asks us to make a commitment to him, to recognize the true value of riches that endure forever. . . ."

The sermon is vintage Stu Phillips, who seeks to walk by faith and in daily commitment to Christ. His worship style is markedly different from his friends at the Lord's Chapel, who listen to Pastor Billy Ray Moore just three miles away.

Nevertheless, Stu is committed to the same evangelical faith, the atonement of Christ, and the work of the Holy Spirit: "There has never been a time in my life when God didn't have his hand on me, yet over the past several years a change has come into my life which I believe is the work of the Holy Spirit. Certain things are more important to me. I'm more relaxed. I know that God has his hand on me more than ever."

About his life in Montreal where his father was an architect, he says, "We grew up as Anglicans surrounded by Roman Catholics. Our church, St. George's, is one of the oldest churches in Montreal. My parents were there every time the doors opened. I was an acolyte, started in the boys' choir when I was six or seven, and later taught Sunday school. I also became a lay elder and an usher. Even when I couldn't attend, I always kept a close association with my church."

Stu became involved in music early. At age eight he bought his own guitar for $8.50 and taught himself to play. Idolizing Gene Autry, he fantasized riding the western ranges to challenge the bad men.

When Stu was thirteen, Gene Autry came to Montreal for a rodeo and amateur talent contest. Stu entered the singing competition and won the first prize of fifteen dollars. The officials were so impressed that they took up a collection which netted Stu $150.

After attending Sir George Williams College in Montreal, he moved to the western prairies and worked as a radio announcer for CFRN, Edmonton. He did the sign-on show, "Stu for Breakfast," on weekday mornings, as well as station breaks and commercials for other programs. Sunday mornings, when he had to work, he listened to ministers of every denomination. "Even there," he recalls, "God had his hand on my life."

Named the outstanding announcer for Edmonton, he advanced to emceeing a weekly two-hour talent show, produced "The Canadian Opry," and handled many other variety shows. One summer he even filled in as a replacement for the star of "Finian's Rainbow." In Edmonton he met his future wife, Aldona, a Lithuanian girl from the Alberta prairies.

In 1962 Stu went national with a television cowboy variety show. For the next five years he starred on his own "Red River Jamboree" over the Canadian Broadcasting Corporation network. Wearing a Stetson, fancy boots, and six guns for the role, he did rope tricks with his horse, Nugget. During this time he traveled coast to coast in both the United States and Canada, appearing on the Grand Ole Opry in Nashville about forty times.

In 1967 the CBC offered him a dream lifetime contract. He says he turned it down "because I felt the time had come for me to change my cowboy image. I remember distinctly taking my hat off for the last time, pulling my boots off, and hanging up my gunbelts. I've never worn a ten-gallon hat or guns since."

Joining the Opry in 1967, he moved to Nashville with his wife, Aldona, and their two children, Leagh and Joel. Today Leagh is a stewardess for TWA; Joel is a premed student at Middle State Tennessee University. A third son, Jasson, born in Nashville, is still in grade school.

In 1975 Stu, taking another turn in his life, began preparation to become an Episcopal worker priest, while continuing on the Opry. Now having completed his studies, he's not entirely sure of what his future holds: "I can be happy as a pastor with a special ministry to people in the entertainment world. But then, maybe the Lord will open a door for me to use my broadcasting experience in Christian television."

He tries to keep his ecclesiastical and entertaining roles separate: "In the church and on the Opry, I try to do everything for the glory of God. I'll go along with being introduced as an Episcopal priest on the Opry. But I don't think it's my place to say, 'Well, folks, as long as I've got you here, open your Bibles to such and such.'

"The Opry isn't a church. I believe you can impose upon people to the detriment of the Word. One of the greatest mistakes in history occurred when Constantine declared Christianity to be the official religion of the Roman Empire. People didn't really change. They just fell into a folk culture.

"What's important is that Opry people and my fans know my spiritual position and that my church knows my music position. I don't think anyone should use the Lord for show business."

Stu Phillips, George Hamilton IV, Barbara

Mandrell, Larry Gatlin, Sonny James, Charlie Walker, Kitty Wells, and Wilma Lee Cooper, all worshiping at different churches, express the Christian faith in various ways. Their appearance and their style of dress also differ. However, despite the different tastes they appeal to along the country music spectrum, they and other Christians in country music try to make God the most important Person in their lives. That's the similarity which really counts.

Ryman Auditorium, home of the Grand Ole Opry for years, is popularly known as the "Mother Church of Country Music." *(Photo by J. Hefley)*

Hank Snow performs on
the Grand Ole Opry stage.
(Photo by J. Hefley)

The Reverend Jimmie Snow, son of
superstar Hank Snow, preaches from the
Grand Ole Opry stage. *(Photo by J. Hefley)*

Marijohn Wilkin is best known for "One Day at a Time," written with Kris Kristofferson.

Donna Stoneman, the blonde, dancing mandolin player, went from despair to joy when she found Christ.

The late Tex Ritter, cowboy actor and singer, loved God and his country. *(Photo by Bert Tippett)*

Grandpa Jones turns
'em on at the Opry.
(Photo by J. Hefley)

Connie Smith found
Christ in a TV studio
and lives for him
onstage and off.
(Photo by J. Hefley)

t Boone, native Nashvillean, sings on
mmie Snow's "Grand Ole Gospel Time."
hoto by Bert Tippett)

Billy Grammer wants to be a
witness for God wherever he go[es]

Jerry Clower and Skeeter Davis backstage at the Opry. *(Photo by J. Hefley)*

Jerry Clower, country comic and devoted man of God, says he wants people to remember him as a real person, "praising the Lord" wherever they saw him. *(Photo by Top Billing, Inc.)*

Wilma Lee Cooper, in an up-to-date photo, preparing to go onstage at the Opry. *(Photo by J. Hefley)*

Stoney and Wilma Lee Cooper, with
daughter Carol. Since Stoney's death,
Wilma Lee's been working with her band,
The Clinch Mountain Clan. *(Photo by
Moss Photo Service, Inc.)*

Roy Acuff, "The King of Country Music," and Minnie Pearl, "The Belle of Grinder's Switch," clowning around backstage at the Opry. *(Photo by J. Hefley)*

George Hamilton IV is the first American country singer to perform in Eastern Europe and the Soviet Union. *(Photo by J. Hefley)*

Jeannie C. Riley of "Harper Valley PTA" fame found her life changed for the better when she gave it to God. *(Photo by Bruno of Hollywood)*

Dolly Parton, a puzzle to many, claims she's "extremely religious" but isn't a Christian. "That's because I don't want to set a bad example." *(Photo by J. Hefley)*

Vic Willis, on the right, is one of the newest country music Christians. *(Photo by J. Hefley)*

Koinonia Christian Bookstore & Coffeehouse, meeting place of the new Music City Christian Fellowship. *(Photo by J. Hefley)*

Johnny Cash, music superstar par
excellence, sings in his own unique style.
(Photo by Youth for Christ, U.S.A.)

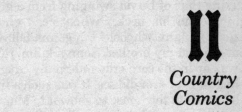

II

Country Comics

It wouldn't be the Opry without Roy Acuff "walking the dog" with his yo-yo onstage or balancing a fiddle bow on the end of his nose, while the crowd oohs in admiration.

Nor without Cousin Minnie Pearl, the "Belle of Grinder's Switch," waltzing across the stage in a green organdy skirt, price tag swinging from her flower-and-vegetable-topped hat. Coquettishly tossing her head and shrieking, "Howdeeee, I'm jist so proud to be here," and then rolling into some humorous lines:

"You know sumpin'? I had my pitcher took. I shore did. I said to the photographer, 'That pitcher doesn't do me justice.'

"And he said, 'Lady, you don't need justice. You need mercy.'

"I'd like to shake hands with all the ladies and kiss all the fellers. I can get the hand shakin' over in a hurry, but the kissin' takes tiiiimmme. I ain't been kissed in so long that I forgit whether you should draw in your breath or blow it out."

Nor without Jerry Clower swooping across the stage in a ruffled yellow shirt and tux, a glittering Star of David swinging from a gold chain around his neck: "Whooooie. I shore feel good tonight. Whoooie! I'm gonna tell you about me and my brother, Sonny, killin' rats. We wuz up in the corn crib and Sonny caught the hugest rat I ever did see. It was such a fine rat he run into the house to show it to Mama.

"Now Sonny didn't know that Reverend Brock, the Baptist preacher, was in the house visitin' Mama. He done rushed into the living room and said, 'Looka here, Mama, at what a rat. I done whupped him over the head with an ear of corn; I done stomped him three or four times. . . .'

"Then Sonny up and saw that preacher. Oh, I'll tell ye, his eyes got big. He hugged that ole rat up to his chest and stroked it and cried. And he said, 'And preacher, the good Lord done called the poor thing home.'"

Then there's the cornspun humor of "Hee-Haw":

"Hey, Grandpa! What's for supper?" yells the chorus, and Grandpa Jones recites:

Vinegar-seasoned collard greens,
A heapin' pot of pinto beans,
Hot buttered cornbread piled in a stack,
And a slice of onion that'll bite you back.

Stay around a little longer, and you'll see 300-pound Junior Savage, all of 5 feet, 6 inches, who plays the "world's greatest car salesman (BR549)" conducting a "lab test" for consumers. You might also hear the latest news from Station KORN and the Reverend Grady Nutt telling another preacher story to the "good ole boys" in the barber shop.

Dumped by a network that didn't think it would succeed, "Hee-Haw" is now in its twelfth year and the most successful syndicated television show in history. Proof of the pudding is Junior Sample's prosperity: "Before 'Hee-Haw,' Grace and I lived in a two-room shack. Now we live in a nice house. We have all the modern conveniences—like indoor plumbing. A rumor started around that I can't read or write. When anybody asks if that is the truth, I tell them I can read well enough to know the amount of my paycheck and write enough to endorse it at the bank."

Junior, heading out for Las Vegas, says, "My agent tells me it will be the first time a performer dressed in bib overalls has ever entertained on a Vegas stage."

And the corn grinds on. What would country music be without the comics?

Dr. Leslie Flynn asks, "Why is it that of all the creatures in the world, only man can laugh? Why, on hearing something funny, does a person throw back his head, open his mouth, and with chest heaving to and fro as though in convulsions, laugh as his breath pumps out in explosive puffs? The answer is because God made him so."

That must be it, for joking and punning have been part of human dialogue ever since the first corn started poppin' in the Garden of Eden.

The lines of Minnie Pearl, Jerry Clower, and the tomfoolery of "Hee-Haw" are straight out of the southern mountains from which so many country musicians have come. The stories heard on the Opry, "Hee-Haw," and the other modern country music shows have been told around countless campfires and house raisings, at innumerable pie suppers and quilting bees, and in numerous circles of whittlers killing time around pot-bellied stoves in general stores when it was too dry for planting or too wet for plowing.

Whether in song, skit, or monologue, the hillbilly humor was about everyday life which the people understood. Many of the stories involved preachers, churches, angels, and Bible characters. Country music fans today are still hearing:

"Didja hear about the two old maids comin' home from church? Dorree said to Saree, 'There shore warn't many in service today.'

"'No, there warn't. When the preacher said, "dearly beloved," I thought he was proposin' to one of us.'"

"The other night I was in a church whar the preacher passed the hat after his sermon. It took a long time, but finally the hat come back with nary a penny. The preacher shook it, turned it upside down, and said, 'Thank Ye, Lord, that I got back my hat from these skin-flints.'"

"Tom Hatfield's little girl asked him, 'Pa, why don't angels have whiskers?'

"'Well, I reckon, it's because they got to heaven by a close shave.'"

"A troublemaker interrupted a preacher's sermon on ole Lot. 'Preacher,' he said, 'do you really believe Lot's wife was turned into a pillar of salt?'

"'When I get to heaven, I'll ask her,' the preacher said.

"'What if she ain't thar?'

"'Then you ask her.'"

The names of musical groups and many of the tunes they sang were enough to elicit smiles. How could an audience keep from grinning when the "Skillet Lickers" took off on "Flop-eared Mule," "Sally, Let Me Chaw Your Rosin Some," and "You Can't Make a Monkey out of Me"? When Uncle Dave Macon, the Dixie Dewdrop, thumped his banjo to "Rabbit in the Pea Patch," "Carve that Possum," or "The Cross-eyed Butcher and the Cacklin' Hen," the crowds revelled in the humor.

The musicians played all the strings of human emotion—from heartbreakers to rib ticklers. One minute a performer would be wailing about "dear old Mother lying . . . in a lonely graveyard . . . 'neath the cold, cold clay." The

next he would be bouncing with "The Old
Hen Cackled and the Rooster's Going to Crow,"
a rather earthy ditty about fowl sex.

Even many of the sad songs had humorous
lines. For example, Alfred Reed's ballad, "How
Can a Poor Man Stand Such Times and Live?"
included a line about "preachers who preach
for dough and not for soul; that's what keeps
a poor man in a hole."

The immediate ancestors of the comics on
today's country music shows rode on the tail-
gates of medicine wagons. Roy Acuff, Jimmie
Rodgers, Gene Autry, Bob Wills, and many
more country music pioneers of the twentieth
century made their first show tours with the
sellers of patent medicine.

Roy Acuff might not be the "King of Country
Music" today had he not traveled a summer
with Dr. Hauer's medicine show out of Knoxville. At the time, Roy was recovering from a
sunstroke which had dashed his hopes of a
professional baseball career.

Dr. Hauer, who lived down the street from
the Acuffs, liked Roy's fiddling and easy ban-
ter. He offered him a dollar a day to fiddle,
sing, and tell jokes. Roy's preacher-father said,
"I always wanted to travel with a medicine
show myself. Go ahead, son, and enjoy yourself."

Roy, Dr. Hauer, and veteran musician Jake
Tindell left Knoxville in Doc's Reo sedan in
the summer of 1932. They played mountain
towns across East Tennessee and Virginia,

performing and peddling patent medicines in county seat squares.

When a crowd gathered, Roy struck up a fast fiddle tune with Jack accompanying on the guitar. Between numbers, they told "Hee-Haw" type jokes and did skits, some of which Roy later used on the Opry. Sometimes Roy blacked up for a minstrel role. Other times he'd mimic an overgrown hillbilly boy, a young girl, or an old mountaineer.

During, and after, the show, Doc gave his pitches. "Step right up, folks. Only one dollar for a bottle of Mocoton Tonic. Guaranteed to cure worms, dyspepsia, sick headaches, constipation, indigestion, pain in the side, back, and limbs, and a torpid liver."

Doc also sold soaps, candy, and a sure cure for corns on toes. To demonstrate, he would pour the stuff over a volunteer's heavy shoes. The brew would seep through the leather and numb the man's feet, making him believe his corns had been dissolved.

Since the thirties every radio country music show has also carried comedians. The most famous outside the Opry have been Lulu Belle and Scotty (Myrtle Cooper and Scott Wiseman) who kept WLS, Chicago, audiences happy for over twenty years. Married on both the stage and in real life, Lulu Belle played a brash, pushy, fussy wife, who picked fights and kept the cheerful Scotty in line.

Every old-time musician had a repertoire of stories and stunts. Of course, Roy Acuff's balancing a fiddle bow on his nose and yo-yoing have become Opry classics. He developed the fiddle bow act by balancing cornstalks in the field when a boy. Eventually he was able to raise a plow in the air, balance it on his chin, and walk around the field with it. His father saw him one day and warned, "Son, you're going to kill yourself if you don't stop that."

When President Richard Nixon came for the opening show in the new Opry house, he pulled a yellow yo-yo from his coat. Dangling it at the end of the string in a futile attempt to imitate Roy, he said, "I haven't learned to use this thing yet." When Roy tried to teach him the art of yo-yoing, the President interrupted him: "Roy, I'll stay here and learn to yo-yo, and you go to Washington and be President."

A familiar sight in floppy hat, overalls, and work shoes is seventy-year-old "Bashful Brother Oswald" (Pete Kirby) imitating Roy's yo-yo with one the size of a tricycle tire. Os, who raises hysterics by clomping with the girl cloggers on the Opry stage, is one of Roy's longest associates.

As a boy, Os learned to play guitar and banjo in his native Smoky Mountains and sold moonshine for his father. After an unsuccessful try at country music in Chicago, Os went home and joined Roy Acuff's Crazy Tennesseans, known today as the Smoky Mountain Boys.

When Roy brought on Rachel Veach, an eighteen-year-old banjo player, they began to get letters asking how she could remain a lady and travel with a bunch of men. One day while they were riding in the car, Os gave his big trademark Ha-ha-ha-ha horselaugh. Roy thought he sounded like a bashful boy and said, "I'm gonna make you Rachel's brother and put you two on as 'Rachel and her great, big, bashful brother Oswald.'" So he did and that stopped the critical mail.

Os and Rachel each had a blackened tooth. Os wore a black wig, checked visor cap, and big britches with suspenders. Rachel wore long bloomers, which kept drooping below her dress, and high-buttoned shoes with white stockings. They laughed, told jokes, sang funny songs, and convulsed crowds.

Oswald drank heavily until 1969 when doctors warned that he would die from liver disease if he didn't stop. He has never touched a drop since, but still uses a half-pint whiskey bottle full of water for his act. He brings on an explosive device called the "smudge pot," loaded with smoke bombs, black gunpowder, and firecrackers.

When Os takes a swig from the bottle, Roy complains about drinking onstage. Then Os spits out the water in a long arc at the smudge pot. Touched off by another band member offstage, the incendiaries explode in a blanket of black smoke.

Besides "bashful brother Oswald," the Opry has had a whole string of comedians, including Uncle Dave Macon, Lonzo and Oscar, Cousin Jody, the Duke of Paducah, Jamup and Honey,

Rod Brasfield, Stringbean Ackeman, and a number of others.

Uncle Dave was mainly a banjo picker, but he could be funny. An old handbill announced:

LOOK WHO'S COMING
UNCLE DAVE MACON & SAM MCGEE
FROM TENNESSEE
FUNNY CLEAN JOKES AND LOTS OF FUN
BRING THE WHOLE FAMILY
15¢ & 25¢

Some of the funniest stories were told on Uncle Dave. One originated in a recording studio where they had trouble with his foot stomping. Someone finally put a pillow under the foot. "Take it away," he ordered. "If I can't hear my foot, I can't hold the rhythm."

Lonzo and Oscar started singing and poking fun at one another and others on the Opry during World War II. Two of their biggest hits were "I'm My Own Grandpa" and "Did You Have to Bring That up While I Was Eating?" The original Oscar still performs, but the act has a third Lonzo (the first withdrew; the second died of a heart attack).

Cousin Jody, a talent on the Dobro (resonated) guitar, started with Roy Acuff. With floppy hat, checkered suspenders, and Purina feed-sack pants, he was a sight when he made his chin touch his nose.

The Duke of Paducah (Whitey Ford) became famous as a teller of tall tales. His trademark close was "I'm headin' for the wagon, boys.

These shoes are killin' me!"

Jamup and Honey, the famous Opry black-face act, were portrayed by Bunny Biggs and Honey Wild, who also played the side characters on the radio: Joe Blow, Firecracker, One Flung, Tuff Stuff Huffman, Pancho, and many others. In days when minstrel acts were acceptable, they were a riot on the Opry.

Rod Brasfield, who flirted with Minnie Pearl onstage, died in 1958. Said the pastor at his funeral: "I expect to see Rod just inside the golden gates and hear him say as he so often asked on the Opry, 'Come on in, Preacher. Where in the cat hair have you been?'"

Stringbean Ackeman, one of the most beloved country comics, grew up as Dave Ackeman on a Kentucky farm and cared for little but banjo picking, baseball, hunting, and fishing. He came to the Opry in 1942 with Bill and Charlie Monroe. A fiddler named him "Stringbean."

On the Opry and later on "Hee-Haw," he wore a low-waisted suit and knocked his knees together in a way which brought the house down. With his sadsack delivery and eyes which flipped up and down like window shades, he was funny on any line.

Stringbean and "Mrs. String," as his wife, Estelle, was called, lived in a little three-room red house near Grandpa and Ramona Jones outside Nashville. Jimmie Snow may have been the only preacher who ever visited them. They were friendly but never dropped in at Evangel Temple.

Stringbean's favorite hobby was fishing. He and Grandpa spent many hours on the lake with neither one saying a word. Stringbean owned twenty Cadillacs but never drove one. "My wife don't tell me how to fish, and I don't tell her how to drive," he often said. He joked about Estelle as "the only woman I know that can swallow a banana sideways," but it was obvious that he loved her deeply. One was seldom seen without the other.

Both carried large amounts of money in their clothing. At 10:20 P.M. on Saturday, November 10, 1974, Stringbean played his banjo and sang, "I'm Going to the Grand Ole Opry and Make Myself a Name." It was to be his last time on the Opry stage.

The next morning when Grandpa Jones went to take Stringbean on a hunting trip to Virginia, he found both Ackemans dead from gunshot wounds. The robbers, waiting for them to come home from the Opry, had attacked them as they were entering the house. The criminals missed $3,300 hidden in a secret pocket on Stringbean's bib overalls and another $2,200 tucked in a tobacco sack pinned inside Estelle's clothing. They were later caught and sentenced to long prison terms. One claimed he had been drinking and smoking marijuana and could not recall what happened.

At the funeral, flower arrangements in the shape of a fish and a steering wheel adorned the caskets. Two hearses rolled side by side at the head of a long funeral procession. "One of the prettiest sights I've ever seen, in spite of the sadness," Roy Acuff said.

"Stringbean," said a mournful Grandpa Jones, "wouldn't have hurt a fly."

"Grandpa" Louis Jones, the "old" fellow with the floppy hat, bushy moustache, baggy pants, suspenders, and rubber boots, was also born in Kentucky. The youngest of ten children in a tenant farm family, he says, "We moved so much that every time the wagon backed up to the door, the chickens laid down and crossed their legs."

As a boy Louis learned to play a guitar brought to work by an employee at a sawmill. When the mill closed, one of his brothers bought him a steel guitar for seventy-five cents at a junk shop. At sixteen he won fifty dollars in a talent contest and was on his way to musical fame.

"My mother told me to get into a good, solid profession—something that would pay me well and last," Grandpa recalls. "I never did like working, so I went into music and comedy."

He got the name "Grandpa" at twenty-two when performing with Bradley Kincaid over a Boston radio station: "I was tired from performing every night and people said I sounded like eighty. So I fixed up with a false moustache. I was the awfulest sight you ever saw. Now I don't need much to make me look the part." Grandpa was sixty-seven in 1980.

During the next seventeen years Grandpa performed on a string of stations. In 1946, the year Grandpa joined the Opry, he met his match in Ramona Riggins, a coal miner's daughter, who played four instruments and sang harmony. Soon after, they got married and have been working together ever since.

Grandpa, who joined "Hee-Haw" in 1969, considers it "one of the greatest things that ever happened to me. I reckon people like to see somebody make a fool of himself."

Grandpa says he "loves to see people laugh, especially children. That's when I think I'm doing a little something worthwhile in this old world. . . . In the old days nearly every show had a slapstick comedian. Most of 'em had a rag around one toe and were called Elmer. . . . I keep trying things 'til I find something that works. If the audience is cold, I may pick out one person and play to him. If I can get just one laughing, it can spread to the whole audience."

For a while Grandpa performed with the old radio team, Lum and Abner, and still uses some of their jokes. He also tells stories about relatives and himself: "I had an uncle who was so bald he had to draw a chalk mark up to here to tell where to wash his face." He freely admits that he's sometimes absent-minded. Once he looked all day over his farm for a cow and then remembered the animal was in his freezer, waiting to be cooked.

He thinks the old-time music is the best: "Some people call me old and dyed-in-the-wool, but I really believe the older style is coming back. A lot of today's country music can't be told from pop."

Grandpa and Ramona recently moved to Mountain View, Arkansas, from which they commute to the Opry and to "Hee-Haw" tapings. Among their friends they're known as solid, God-fearing people who live by the old landmarks. "That way," Grandpa says seriously, "is the *best* way."

Without question, "Hee-Haw" has the most comedians of any country show. The newest member of the cast is the Reverend Grady Nutt, billed as the "Prime Minister of Humor." Nutt—his real name—is a seminary-trained preacher (Southern Baptist Theological Seminary in Louisville) with experience in the pastorate before turning full-time humorist. He says he was pastor of a rural church where "the potholes were so deep in the parking lot you could be baptized in 'em."

Of all the singers and comedians on "Hee-Haw," none has a more dramatic and pathetic story than LuLu Roman, the big girl who can draw laughs by merely rolling her eyes. LuLu's pilgrimage from drugs and wild living to a new life in Christ is related in her recent biography titled *LuLu* (Fleming H. Revell).

LuLu, born Bertha Louise Hable, never knew her father. Her parents were divorced shortly after her birth. Even the relationship with her mother was distant. When she was four, her great-grandmother put her in a Baptist orphan's home in Texas.

She kept expecting her grandmother to come back for her. "She isn't coming," a housemother said sternly. "You're going to live with us now." When LuLu began sobbing, the woman warned, "If you make another sound, I'll blister you." That night LuLu wet the bed and got a severe spanking.

The home operated by very rigid rules; everything—getting up, washing, dressing, eating, marching to school, and sleeping—was programmed by whistles and bells. The housemothers kept close tabs on everyone. The children had to eat everything on their plates. LuLu's only private place was her tiny closet.

It seemed that LuLu was always in trouble. Once when she looked up at a housemother, the insensitive woman shouted at her, "Don't you buck those eyes at me!"

Visitors could come for one hour on Saturday. Church attendance was mandatory on Sunday: two hours in the morning and two hours in the evening. The preachers pounded their Bibles and shook their fingers at the children. At night LuLu lay awake terrified by the thought of dying.

They did allow her to take piano lessons. One day a housemother found her playing "Chopsticks" on the piano with her bare toes. The housemother didn't realize she was only trying to get attention from the girls laughing around her. "No more lessons!" the woman screamed.

When LuLu began helping in the kitchen, she resolved her frustrations by eating. She also loved plays and putting on funny faces at Halloween. She could disguise her face but not the fat body of which she was so ashamed.

LuLu's closest friend, Patty, began slipping out at night. The housemother who had stopped LuLu's piano lessons caught and beat Patty until the blood ran down her legs. Patty had to be hospitalized.

When they reached the tenth grade, the girls were bused outside to a high school where they were teased about being from the home. LuLu learned to smoke. She also began sneaking out at night and became acquainted with drugs.

Upon high school graduation LuLu received fifty dollars, a set of luggage, an outfit of clothing, and a list of job prospects. She and Patty got an apartment and became more heavily involved in drugs. They were both hired as telephone operators, but LuLu became sarcastic with callers. After being warned by her supervisor, she swore at a man placing a long distance call. The phone company fired her and wrote on her employment record: "Not recommended for rehiring."

She then moved in with a couple of ex-residents of the home who were selling drugs, forging checks, and buying merchandise on stolen credit cards. LuLu was caught trying to use a stolen card and put on probation.

Penniless, she roomed with a go-go dancer and got work in a nightclub. Wearing huge clown bloomers, a red bow in her hair and another on her back, she bounced onstage, rolling her eyes and licking a big sucker. The customers went wild. With some of her first earnings, she bought a Continental luxury car.

She fell in love with a man named Harry, who soon moved in with her. One night she came home early and found him in her bed with another girl. When she chased them out, Harry took her new car and left.

"Dear God, get me out of this mess," she prayed. It was the first time she had prayed since the sixth grade.

Then Buck Owen's manager called her unexpectedly. "We're putting together a cornball answer to 'Laugh In,'" he said. 'We want you to be 'Goldie Hawn.'" Meeting her at the Los Angeles airport, Buck and the manager gave her a pink dress with ruffles and big buttons to wear. LuLu was sensational on television.

Later moving to Nashville where the "Hee-Haw" shows were being taped, she spent money wildly, trying to buy attention and friendship. She bought another Continental and furnished a new home with psychedelic posters and astrological charts. Harry returned, begging forgiveness. He moved back in; then when he discovered she was pregnant, he left.

When police caught her with five-and-a-half pounds of marijuana, she was dropped from "Hee-Haw." A lawyer was able to get the marijuana possession charge dismissed, and she moved to Dallas.

Pregnant and desperate, she took an overdose of pills, turned up her stereo, and lay down to die. A friend came by just in time.

When her baby was born, the doctor told

her he would not make it through the night. LuLu again cried out to God. The baby survived, but LuLu went back to selling drugs.

Patty's little sister Diane came to see her. "I want to help you," she said. "I love you. Jesus wants to help you. He loves you."

For several months Diane and another friend cared for LuLu and the baby, paid the rent, and bought groceries. LuLu reluctantly agreed to go with them to the Beverly Hills Baptist Church.

About a month later she asked Diane to take her to Pastor Howard Conatser's study. The pastor talked to her in simple terms and then asked her, "Will you go on carrying this load or will you lay it at the foot of the cross?" They knelt while LuLu said a simple sinner's prayer. She got up feeling lighter; all the way home she kept shouting, "Praise the Lord!"

During the next few months she basically went nowhere except to church. Christian friends helped her care for the baby. Then a church asked her to give her testimony. One invitation led to another. Soon she was speaking to churches and youth crusades across the country and making television appearances.

At the "Hee-Haw" offices, she told her old friends about the change in her life. Before she left, they asked her to return to the show.

Every week millions of "Hee-Haw" fans see LuLu smiling and making eyes, doing comedy skits, and sometimes singing a hymn of testimony.

If you visited her home, the first thing you'd

notice are the butterflies. Carved from wood, spun from gossamer and etched on metal, they are all over her house. She says they're a symbol of what happened to her. Like them, she onced lived in a shell and groveled in the dirt until emerging with God's help, she was given wings to fly.

The one and only Minnie Pearl, "Aunt Minnie" to the girls on "Hee-Haw," entertains Opry audiences almost every Friday and Saturday night. Her background is almost the opposite of LuLu's.

Born Ophelia Sarah Colley, the youngest of five sisters, she was reared in a warm, loving, church-going family in the small town of Centerville, Tennessee, about fifty miles southwest of Nashville.

Ophelia appeared in her first recital at three, but she gave her most memorable performance two years later when she and a little cousin were to carry their aunt's bridal train in a society wedding. Everything went fine at the dress rehearsal. The next evening as the bride was moving toward the altar to the tune of "The Wedding March," little Ophelia suddenly dropped her end of the train, sat down on the floor, and began crying loudly. The wedding was thrown into confusion. Mrs. Colley rushed to her child's side: "What's wrong, honey? Tell Mother."

"Oh, Mama," Ophelia wailed. "I'm not gonna do this again. Auntie was married last night."

Ophelia survived the wedding. She also

went on to become a popular girl in high school. She made good grades, was a cheer leader and an expert tennis player, and always had plenty of dates.

Her parents sent her to Ward-Belmont College, a Baptist girls' school, attended by the finest young women of central Tennessee. Graduating in dramatics during the Depression, she returned home to Centerville to teach high school.

She quit teaching school to travel the Southeast, helping an Atlanta firm produce amateur shows for civic clubs. She met "Minnie Pearl" in an Appalachian mountain town. Ophelia says, "This woman treated me so beautifully and was so funny and told the wildest tales that I came away talking like her."

Later Ophelia stopped at a resort hotel in South Carolina and was asked to help with a benefit show—maybe dressing up in an old gingham dress and doing a routine. Agreeing to do it, she bought a bright yellow dress for $1.98, a pair of flat-heeled slippers, white stockings, and a flat straw hat decked with fruits and flowers.

"Howdeeee," she called to the well-dressed crowd at the benefit. "I'm jist so glad to be here. This here's Minnie Pearl. That's my name, 'Minnie Pearl,' it is." The dignified guests laughed themselves silly.

When her father died, she went home to help support her mother. Taking a job with the WPA, she managed a recreation program for children. The future in dramatics for

Ophelia and "Minnie Pearl" seemed bleak. She felt she was a failure at twenty-eight.

About a year later in 1939, the Tennessee Banking Association at Centerville invited her to do her "Minnie Pearl" act. She impressed Nashville banker Bob Turner, who recommended her to the Opry. WSM gave her an audition but feared the resentment of some people who might feel she was putting them down. Nevertheless, WSM let her perform at 11:05 P.M. Saturday when much of the Opry crowd would be gone and little harm would be done if she failed. Her initial performance, for which she received ten dollars, brought in over 250 fan letters and a bid to join the Opry as a permanent member.

Since then "Minnie Pearl" has appeared abroad and in almost every major American city and television variety show, as well as performing on the Opry for forty years. Ophelia says, "'Minnie Pearl' is just a lil' ole country gal who comes to town to flirt with the fellers, but nothing serious or she'd run all the way back to the farm."

She sticks to the old jokes which audiences never seem to outgrow:

"I know this ole boy back home in Grinder's Switch. When he's told you 'Howdy,' he's told you all he knows."

"Feller said to me the other day, 'Minnie, you look just like a breath of spring.' Wal, he didn't quite say that. What he said was, 'You look like the end of a hard winter.'"

"Brother went into a blacksmith shop the other day and picked up a hot horseshoe and dropped it right off. 'Burned ya, didn't it?' the blacksmith said.

"'Nope,' Brother told him. 'It just don't take me long to look at a horseshoe.'"

"And there's my Uncle Nabob. He's no failure. He just started at the bottom and liked it there."

Ophelia is married to lawyer Henry Cannon, who manages her business affairs and is an expert pilot who used to fly her to show dates. Often accompanying her to the Opry, Henry stands admiringly just offstage while "Minnie Pearl" takes over.

The Cannons have a beautiful Brentwood home with a swimming pool and tennis courts. They are involved in the Nashville community and in the Methodist Church. Ophelia has frequently been asked to lend her name and energies to worthy causes. She has served, for example, as Honorary Chairman of the Tennessee Cancer Crusade and as Chairman of Heart Sunday also in Tennessee.

A humble woman, Ophelia Cannon gives God the credit for directing her life: "I always wanted to be an actress, but the Lord never intended for me to go in that direction, because he knew I didn't have the talent. The Lord gave me 'Minnie Pearl' and this sense of humor to make a few people laugh and ease a few burdens in an aching world."

If "Minnie" has a male counterpart on the Opry, it would be Jerry Clower, the whooping, howling, yarn-spinning ex-fertilizer salesman from Yazoo City, Mississippi. One difference is that the "275-pound canary—whut is the Opry's heaviest act," is the same person on, and off, the stage.

Some people will tell you that Jerry is the most respected Christian in country entertainment. A Nashville preacher's wife who is close to a lot of Opry people says, "Jerry's the only man I know who can come up and hug a woman on the street and cause no suspicion. He just naturally loves everybody and everybody knows he has one of the best marriages in show business."

The year he turned forty-three, he was making $17,000 selling fertilizer for the Mississippi Chemical Corporation in Yazoo City; the next year he was bringing in $200,000 "for tellin' stories funny."

Jerry remembers when he first realized that he had become a big-time entertainer. "I was a settin' in a motel room a readin' the *Nashville Banner* and there was a pitcher of me and Tammy Wynette. They was a callin' both of us 'country music stars.' I said to myself, 'A star. Why, I'm forty-four years old.' I phoned my wife in Yazoo City and said, 'Dahlin', my soul, somethin's a happenin' to us. But I want you to know that you're still the main-most woman in my life.'"

Jerry, who never forgets important dates, says that was the year his wife, Homerline, then forty-four, became pregnant: "After Ray, Amy, and Sue comin' so many years before, we never figured on Katy. We had a lot more faith in that man goin' to the moon than we did in Mama ever comin' up pregnant. We thought our crop was laid by. Katy's the most precious thing God ever did for us."

Jerry also remembers when he first saw Homerline: "It was at a revival meeting, the Thursday night before the fourth Sunday in July in 1939. We both publicly professed our faith in Christ and were baptized in the East Fork of the Amite River on Sunday. She was the most beautiful thing I'd ever seen." She was also in the third grade and Jerry never looked twice at another girl.

Jerry says, "She's always been my number one. If God gave me the ingredients to make a woman, I'd make her just like Homerline. I praise God for her every day."

Jerry's own parents were divorced when he was a baby. He and his brother, Sonny, lived with their mother, who remarried when Jerry was thirteen. The brothers grew up milking cows, rounding up calves, playing 'gator in the creek and Tarzan in the trees, hunting coons and possums, going to school (he didn't miss a day in twelve years), and attending church twice on Sunday and once in the middle of the week.

During World War II Jerry served in the Navy and earned three battle stars. When he came home, he attended Mississippi State University where he became an outstanding football lineman. He says, "The first college football game I ever saw was the one I played in."

With a degree in agriculture he served as an assistant county agent and then went to work for the Mississippi Chemical Company as a traveling fertilizer salesman.

After a few years he decided he was talking too much about fertilizer and not telling enough funny stories. That's when he started his famous coon hunt yarn which friends insisted he record. "Jerry Clower from Yazoo City, Mississippi, Talkin'" sold half a million and launched his new career.

The coon story, which he still tells 200 times a year, is about the tree-top confrontation occurring when professional tree climber John Eubanks shinnies up the tallest sweet gum tree in southern Mississippi to dislodge what he thinks is a tree raccoon. It turns out to be a lynx, or as Jerry says, "a souped-up wildcat." The story continues:

"'Waaaaaaooooooh! This thang's a killin' me,' John yelled while the whole top of the tree was shakin' and the dogs were bitin' the bark off the tree and a fightin' one another. 'Wooooo, shoot this thang!'

"The fella on the ground yelled back, 'Joohnnn, I can't shoot up in thar. I might hit you.'

"'Well, jist shoot up in heah amongst us,' John screamed. 'One of us has got to have some relief.'"

The coon story has made Jerry over a million dollars.

Onstage, Jerry doesn't simply talk when he tells a funny story. He bellows, wails, howls, screeches, contorts his face, furrows his brow, and puckers his lips. He also imitates a chain saw, a diesel truck, a motorcycle, and a Brahman bull.

He's never been known to tell an off-color story: "It's a challenge to make people laugh with clean, nonrisqué humor. I've proven that you can make it without being vulgar or obscene." Jerry also says there's no secret to his ability to make people laugh: "It's the joy within what comes from knowin' Jesus Christ."

In addition to the Opry, variety shows, and hundreds of conventions, Jerry has probably appeared on every television talk show in the country: "I have my Christian convictions, but I try to be careful not to alienate myself from everyone. I don't want anyone in television to say, 'Let's don't get him back, for all he wants to do is preach.'"

It's practically impossible to rile Jerry, who admits "gettin' a little irritated when I'm asked if I got religion after I became wealthy or before when it was less convenient. Most people whut ask that kind of question has goatees."

Jerry also gets a little upset with people who say one can't live a Christian life and succeed as an entertainer. He replies, "Look at me. I'm a G-rated comic performing in an X-rated world. I don't lie, cheat, swear, smoke, drink, or chew. There ain't no X-rated comic whut has sold as many albums as I have. I think I'm livin' proof that you can live by your convictions and get along good."

Jerry has been named "Country Comedian of the Year" two years in a row by *Billboard, Cash Box,* and *Record World.* But his biggest honor came when he was installed as a member of the Grand Ole Opry. The governor of Mississippi came up for the installation.

Jerry recalls, "When I was a little boy, we used to go on Saturday night to whoever's house had the strongest battery radio and turn on the Opry. We'd turn it loud and hear Mr. Acuff singing, and we'd snatch the knobs off so nobody could move it from WSM. I want to tell you I loved the Opry. And now I'm a member of it! And I'm just a professional talker. I don't do any pickin' or singin' at all. And for all these people to accept me and love me and let me love them, well, that's just overwhelmin'!"

Jerry doesn't live in Nashville. When not traveling, he's at home in Yazoo City where he's a deacon and a lay preacher at the First Baptist Church. Homerline teaches an eleven-year-old girls' Sunday school class there. The rule in their home has always been automatic church attendance. "Nobody need ask," says Jerry. They also tithe Jerry's professional income. The tithe amounts to much more than Jerry made before he put the coon story on record.

Jerry's Christian beliefs have changed his

ideas about racial segregation. "I'm a redneck, but I'm an educated redneck. I was taught that you should never have your mind so made up that facts couldn't change it. The Lord pricked my conscience, and I changed my mind. I'm a Southern liberal now when it comes to civil rights. I'm proud that all our kids went to integrated public schools—I'm most proud that Walter Cronkite came to our town to find where desegregation was workin' in the South. I know some churches which hide clubs and sticks outside the front door so if unwelcome people show up, they can be clubbed down."

Above all, Jerry wants to be known "as a Christian entertainer who performed on, and off, the stage, and folks didn't have to figure out what kind of a mood he was in to approach him. I'd like for people to say, 'Well, ole Jerry, wherever you saw him, he was praising the Lord. And he was Jerry Clower—the Christian comic—twenty-four hours a day.'"

12

*Country Music
Isn't What
It Used to Be*

Jimmie Rodgers' first royalty check amounted to twenty-seven dollars, representing the sale of 6,000 records in a three-month period. Fifty-two years later, in 1980, country record sales racked up $437,000,000. Only rock and roll sold more. For the first time, country music edged ahead of pop.

Shortly after the 1980 totals had been reported, Dolly Parton signed a contract to perform at a Reno supper club and gambling palace for $350,000 a week. What a change from the humble Dolly who'd worn rags and remnants as a child, who'd been raised in a house with "four rooms and a path," and whose father had been a moonshiner. Oddly enough, in 1978 she had been voted one of the ten worst-dressed women in America—"too many yards of Dolly poured into too few inches of fabric"—but not for wearing rags.

It's no accident that Nashville trails New York as the second leading city in the nation for trading stocks and bonds. Tree International, the largest music publishing company on Music Row, is valued at $40 million. Real estate is also high. Half a million paid for a house by a country music star in Brentwood or on the shores of Old Hickory Lake raises no eyebrows.

Roy Acuff, who didn't get his first $100 gate receipts until 1940, is one of those who admits being a millionaire, though he will not say by how much. Owner of a plantation-style home on the Cumberland River and business property in downtown Nashville, he has half-interest in the music publishing company which holds rights to all of Hank Williams' songs.

Being a prudent man, the "King of Country Music" already has his gravestone in place, a sixteen-by-eight-foot, silver gray Georgian marble monument, weighing 13,500 pounds. Sculpted on it are a fiddle, a bow, and a sheet of music; there is also a Grecian urn with an eternal flame. Roy is doing well financially, but there are probably a dozen others in the Nashville music business who are worth more.

Not every one involved in country music is so well-off. There are plenty whose names or clients are not in lights and who still drive used Chevrolets and Fords and pay for their washing machines on the installment plan.

However, it's as plain as the rhinestones on Hank Snow's jacket that the country music industry is booming.

Nashville is simply the hub. Those 6,000 disc jockeys attending the October deejay convention each year in Nashville come from elsewhere. Little Nashvilles are springing up all around the country. One doesn't have to live in Tennessee's capital city any longer to make it big. Bakersfield, California, is not called "Buckersfield" (for Buck Owens' properties) without good reason. Texas isn't doing poorly making cowboy boots and hats either.

The really big money is in Hollywood and network television. Country singers were often featured in many films during the era of "Westerns." Kris Kristofferson and Dolly Parton are today's big moneymakers in the film industry. Either one can make more money in a single picture than some of the old-time country singers earned in a lifetime from records and personal appearances.

The temptation of mega-bucks is understandable, yet the compromises of these stars, particularly Kris Kristofferson, have been disappointing to many Christian fans. They wonder how Kristofferson, who once made a strong Christian profession, can play the roles that he does. How can he apparently condone the immorality of Hollywood?

Country music has indeed come a long way from the hoedowns (square dances) of the twenties and the thirties and from the roadside honky-tonks of the forties and the fifties. Larry Gatlin singing "Take Me to Your Lovin' Place" and the resurrected Hank Williams moaning "I'm So Lonesome I Could Cry" can be heard on loud stereos and passing cars as you walk along almost any street.

But besides the dollars, the jobs, and the entertainment, how influential is country music? Says Arthur Smith, "What the songs of today say influences the country more than the laws. Music is that important. It influences our youth."

Who is Arthur Smith? Not one of the Nashville elite, but the country music czar in Charlotte, North Carolina. He's written "probably a thousand songs," has a television show on over thirty stations, and is in the song publishing business with Johnny Cash. Arthur, also a Southern Baptist deacon and Sunday school teacher, was named "Layman of the Year" by the Southern Baptist Theological Seminary Foundation. "The most real thing in my life has been Christ," he says.

Arthur Smith is among several in the industry seriously concerned about the negative influence much of today's country music is having on youth and society. After all, Chicago critic Gary Deeb calls country music "the most sensuous form of American popular music. For sheer sensuality and overt appeal to sexual interests, there's nothing more racy on the air."

Paul Harvey, who was a teenage deejay, goes further: "Historically, country music reflected apple pie patriotism, virtue, boy-girl romance. Much of today's potage is downright porno."

Is the criticism unfair? A sample of some

recent hits does indicate a preoccupation with sexual themes: Reba McEntire with "You Lift Me up to Heaven When You Lay Me Down" and Ronnie McDowell with "How Far Do You Want to Go?" Roy Clark doesn't want a "piece of paper"—just his girl to love him for "love's own sake." Dolly Parton compares her body to a "Bargain Store," while Larry Gatlin will "Walk a Mile to Love Sweet Becky Walker."

Jack Greene and Jeannie Seely (with deep, plunging neckline) declare, "My love is yours for the taking, so take me. . . ." Marty Robbins, with his shirt unbuttoned almost to his belt buckle, sings Ronnie Millsap's song about "having day dreams about night things in the middle of the afternoon."

Many songs deal with the age-old struggle between morality and sexual infidelity. The latter is usually the most inviting, as with "Heaven's Just a Sin Away." Another catchy one starts with a boy being led into the water to be baptized and the preacher asking, "Do you want to go to heaven?"

"Yes, just lead me on," the boy replies. The song narrative moves to a bar where our hero eyes a woman who has a glass of wine, some time, and a come-on. The preacher's words, "Do you want to go to heaven?" have become faint in the boy's ears.

Turn on any country music station, almost anywhere, anytime, and make your own test. Take Chattanooga, about as conservative a town as you can find. WDOD, "the country music station," aired in succession Glen Campbell's inviting lyrics, "When you're lying next to me, just love me every which way you can"—about an affair between two people not married to each other; another song, "Let's Git It While the Gittin's Good"; and then, "She Was Wild and She Was Willing."

You can sum up the music in one word: SEX and almost always the kind which was once considered immoral, but which, in today's world, has become almost a badge of honor. As Don Williams, who "believes in love," observes, "I don't believe virginity is as common as it used to be."

The Statler Brothers ask, "Whatever happened to Randolph Scott?" and to the old cowboy movies in which honor and justice always prevailed. And whatever happened to the sweet, and bittersweet, country music love ballads which stopped short of the bedroom door while the sinner always paid a price for following the siren call of infidelity?

Roy Acuff, Billy Grammer, Sonny James, Johnny Cash, Stu Phillips, and a few others still sing the old love ballads. With the exception of Cash's songs, you may have to phone in a special request, for deejays tend to replay only the records at the top of the chart. Most artists who cling to the old traditional songs haven't been held in high regard for several years.

The honky-tonk, cheating song era began around 1950. Jimmie Wakely and Margaret Whiting came along with "One Has My Name— The Other Has My Heart" and "Slipping

286

Around." Webb Pierce hit with "Back Street Affair" in which adultery appeared honorable. Other songs of like genre followed as record companies took the cue. Many songs openly appealed to male chauvinists; in morality songs the bad girls usually led the man astray.

Women didn't really get their say until Kitty Wells hit with "It Wasn't God Who Made Honky-Tonk Angels." Loretta Lynn came along in the early sixties with a trio of breakthroughs: "Don't Come Home a Drinkin' with Lovin' on Your Mind" about a man who neglected his wife and came home drinking with sex as his only interest; "Another Man Loved Me Last Night" about a woman cheating on a man who'd been cheating on her; and "The Pill" about the new freedom of a woman who could enjoy sex without fear of getting pregnant. Some stations banned all three records, which a lot of preachers turned into grist for sermons. Record company promoters turned the three into big moneymakers and helped propel Loretta to stardom.

Kitty Wells, who doesn't care for explicit sex in songs, said as late as 1976: "If a woman had sung songs like Loretta's twenty years ago, she'd have been taken out and tarred and feathered."

As Loretta consistently hit the top of the charts, the songs got bolder and bolder. Other artists have gone far beyond her so that today Loretta seems quite square. Still refusing to dress in sexy costumes, she insists that in over twenty-five years of marriage she "ain't never cheated on Doo," her husband. Loretta believes soap operas, not country music, "are the ruination of America."

Some are also concerned that country music is losing its instrumental simplicity. Some of the older performers don't care for the drums and the cymbals which were once banned from the Opry. Rock and roll took care of that. Tolerant Roy Acuff, who says he has "nothing against drums," can "beat a rhythm on a number two tomato can." He says, "Rhythm is the basic element of music, but it shouldn't drown out the sweetness of the melody."

Controversy over crossover has raged for several years. The purists dislike country singers doing pop and pop singers meddling with country. Let the two remain separate, they say. But the crossovers continue, and it's often hard to say whether a song is country or pop; many are a combination.

What really rankles performers like Grandpa Jones, Billy Grammer, Stu Phillips, and Jerry Clower are the questionable lyrics.

Grandpa Jones says, "Too many writers are turning out skin songs and not the gentle, down-to-earth music. When rock and roll came in, I went out. All of it kind of runs in circles, I think. We're going back to the old-time stuff."

Everyone remembers Billy Grammer's little speech on the Opry about smutty songs a number of years ago. The week before the speech, Billy had had a verbal run-in with a Miami deejay who refused to play Billy's new record, "Family Man." The deejay told Billy that if the song had more sexual connotations, it would sell and he would play it. "I got kinda mad," Billy told Nashville reporter Bill Hance.

Still steaming when his turn came to perform on the Friday night Opry, Billy told the audience, "Country music is becoming a smutty word. It doesn't need to be this way. I don't like it. In order for a country song to be popular these days, it has to have lyrics about lying in bed with someone and getting them pregnant before they get married." When Billy stopped, there was a moment's stony silence; then the crowd erupted into a thunderous ovation. The national wire services picked up Billy's remarks and quoted him in newspapers across the country. The Opry management told him to remember that he had a captive audience. "I know," Billy said, "and I'll refrain in the future."

Reflecting on the incident, Billy says that if one of the Opry artists became a Moonie and started talking about it onstage, he and others wouldn't like it. In light of that, he feels he doesn't have the right to put WSM and the Opry on the spot.

"Still, we've got to speak up somehow. Somebody has got to put down some guidelines. I wish the Opry would. I know they're concerned.

"Some people in our industry will tell you people want the sex and the four-letter words. One star told me that this was the 'in' thing. I don't agree."

Stu Phillips says, "Entertainers can have a

tremendous influence on people, just as Gene Autry did on me. It was a nice, clean influence. Nowadays a different image is presented.

"It's the same with television. The way I see things now, people are getting tired of the cheap sex and the way standards are flouted. Several church groups are talking of boycotts, hitting the sponsors of objectionable programs by not buying their products. I don't think those boycotts are going to change society overnight, but they're an indication of how people are becoming fed up. We've seen minorities organize to accomplish certain goals. Special interest groups can arouse the masses. I think these boycotts can be very, very effective.

"Writing letters can help. I know that letters have an impact on me. The country music industry right now is very sensitive to letters. There's a lot of discussion in our circles about providing good, clean family entertainment in country shows. I really believe this country is on the advent of some sort of reformation, but the record company executives will be the last to know.

"We can get the attention of the record companies by our buying habits. About a year ago I bought a small foreign car. I love this country. It's done a lot for me. Buying that car was the only way I had of telling Detroit that they had to change."

Jerry Clower agrees with Stu that those who don't like bad music should put their money where their mouths are: "Sure, I'm concerned about the risqué words and their influence on people. The folks that can control that are the folks that buy the records."

Joe Babcock, a Baptist Sunday school teacher and one of the most versatile and gifted persons in the country music field, declares that "Christians could stop it in a week. No other group can boast 50 percent of the population. If just a small percentage of us would tell the radio and television stations we don't like the songs they're playing and tell the record companies that we aren't going to buy records that glamorize illicit sex and use language we don't like, then something would happen. I include the record companies because they want to make music that people will buy. As long as people buy these records which I find objectionable, I can't say, 'Don't put them out.'"

Joe, a music major graduate of the University of Nebraska, was raised a Baptist but did not commit himself to Christ until he was twenty-five. He says that in 1958 he "decided to make it in music or die trying. I promised the Lord that if he would let me get into the music business, I would never abuse it."

For about a year Joe lived in his car in Southern California and sang from the back of a truck for five dollars for three hours at supermarket openings. In 1959 he went to Nashville to sing with a backup group for Marty Robbins. He left Marty in 1965 "to see if I could write." He hit with "I Washed My Hands in Muddy Water," which Stonewall

Jackson popularized on the Opry. He also wrote "Prairie Fire," "Doggone Cowboy," "Dusty Winds," and "If I Could Cry," which Marty recorded.

Besides writing and singing, Joe is a member of the "Nashville Additions," the backup singers on "Hee-Haw." The "Additions" are one of three or four groups most in demand for recording sessions around Nashville.

Joe recently started a record company, Independent Artists, for recording and marketing "music in good taste." His first album, "Montage," consists of ten songs in five different styles: two cowboy, two country, two contemporary, two comedy, and two gospel.

"We're not in this just to make money," Joe declares. "This is really a crusade to give people more of a choice."

Many more performers are concerned about the trend to compromise both the musical style and the lyrics of country music. As far back as 1974, Hank Snow, Roy Acuff, Vic Willis, Grandpa Jones, and several other traditionalists organized ACE, the Association of Country Entertainers to deal with these and other problems in the industry. A code of ethics guides the behavior of its own members; whenever a performer begins stepping out of line, ACE moves in.

ACE is also zeroing in on the problem of radio stations playing only the top forty or fifty records on the charts. The play list or "stack" of records, which deejays keep at their elbows, is the critical point, according to Opry performer Vic Willis, a board member and former executive director of ACE: "Country stations narrow their lists to forty or fifty records which they play repeatedly. As a result, it's nearly impossible for many new artists, as well as established performers, to get their records aired. Record purchasers buy the songs they hear and deejays select records which sell. It's a vicious cycle which we're trying to break. We've had fans tell us they called stations and were told, 'Well, the records you want are not on the stack.'"

Because of this practice, Vic thinks, many of the best-loved Opry entertainers who refuse to do questionable songs have not been in the top thirty or forty for several years: "But we've got 4,400 people who fill the Opry House three times a week to hear these old 'has beens.' They and their fans deserve better than what they're getting."

ACE has been asking fans to bombard the radio stations and complain about this discriminatory practice. Says Vic: "If people will simply say no to dirty lyrics and complain loud enough, something can be done. People have more power than entertainers. There are only a few hundred of us. There are millions of fans."

13

The Spirit Keeps Moving

Almost 100 years have passed since the colorful Sam Jones invaded Nashville. If the old firebrand were back today, he'd probably have a few choice words to say about Nashville's 594 churches, its religious publishing houses, and its prosperous gospel singers and quartets. He'd have even more to say about the boudoir ballads and hymns sung interchangeably by the same voices, the nudie joints, the wheeling and dealing in the Tennessee legislature, and the record rates of alcohol consumption, divorce, abortion, and murder.

Of course Nashville is similar to other American cities of comparable size. It also happens to be a more obviously religious expression of Bible-belt culture.

What would Sam say about Dolly Parton's religion, which she has freely discussed on television talk shows and in the pages of *Playboy, Penthouse, Playgirl,* and dozens of less controversial magazines and newspapers? "I'm extremely religious," Dolly has told the *San Antonio Express*. "I'll always be that way. But I don't claim to be a Christian, and that's because I don't want to set a bad example.

"I pray every day. Normally, I don't get down on my knees or anything; it's just in my mind. Sometimes I do get on my knees if I feel it's necessary to pray about something that's really sincere. . . . God gives me courage and helps me. I'm not afraid of God. I can joke with him.

"I never make a decision about business or anything without talking to God about it. And usually when I do, I feel after I pray that I've got my answer.

"The way I look at God," she informed *Playboy*, "is . . . he means something different to everybody. We are all God's children."

Dolly, whose grandfather is a Church of God preacher, has been to Evangel Temple and its altar at least once. But she doesn't go to church anymore.

"Carl [her stay-at-home husband whom she met at the Wishy-Washy Laundromat on her first visit to Nashville and who was once mistaken for her gardener] and I are probably afraid we'll become total Christians," she told *Playboy*. In interviews Dolly insists that she is absolutely faithful to Carl, who has never been interviewed or photographed for publication.

Then there's Loretta Lynn, who says she

has "always been religious in my own way."
What would Sam Jones think of her? Back in
Butcher Hollow, Loretta attended church every
Sunday and heard Preacher Elzie Banks. She
recalls, "I believed it all, but for some reason I
was never baptized. After I started in music, I
got away from going to church and reading
the Bible."

Loretta was startled by the change in John
Thornhill, the bass player in her band. After
John got baptized, she noticed he was a different person—studying the Bible on their bus
and praying. Finally she began studying with
him. "I'm going to heaven because I don't
drink or blackguard or run around," she told
John, who insisted she had to be baptized
also.

In 1972 after a couple of trips to the hospital,
Loretta decided to get baptized. She had the
preacher-uncle of her daughter-in-law immerse
her in a Church of Christ tank.

Continuing to be one of the most straight-
laced women in country music ("there ain't
much spicy to tell about me"), she is, nevertheless, enamored with the occult. She reads
palms and some say, can tell fortunes from
the grounds in a coffee cup. She also embraces
the doctrine of reincarnation and believes that
she was an Indian woman and an Irish
dancer in her previous lives.

Sam Jones might also be puzzled by Con-
way Twitty, who often sings with Loretta
Lynn. A local Southern Baptist preacher calls
Conway "one of the great contradictions in

this town. He's one of the worst when it comes to offensive songs, but he's active in a Southern Baptist church and is well known for helping people. The other night I was at the hospital to see my son who was a patient. There was Conway going up and down the halls, visiting people. He puzzles me, yet sometimes I think he's a better Christian than others who go to our churches."

It would be difficult, if not impossible, to find a country musician who will admit to being an atheist. Even Willie Nelson, "the outlaw," claims he is now "more religious than I ever was." Still, it seems that only a small percentage are active in Nashville churches; this is especially true of those who claim membership in mainline Protestant churches: Baptist, Methodist, Presbyterian, and Episcopal.

Of the 131 Southern Baptist churches in the Nashville Baptist Association, only Forest Hills Baptist seems to have had a successful outreach to performers and songwriters—that was several years ago when Bob Daughtery was pastor there. He has since left to become a foreign missionary.

The pressures on the Reverend Jimmie Snow have declined. His much publicized divorce of 1972 is seldom brought up anymore. A bumper sticker on the back of his aging Chrysler reads, "Christians aren't perfect, just forgiven." For speaking engagements, he now has a private plane, which he flies in order to spend more time at home with his family.

Several members of the music community who left Evangel Temple after Jimmie's divorce have returned. Jimmie and the church continue "Grand Ole Gospel Time" after the Friday night Opry. Every Friday night from forty to fifty country music fans make decisions for Christ. Since the program began, the tally has passed 12,000, not including hundreds of radio listeners who have indicated their professions of faith by letter. Jimmie has received a prestigious Religious Heritage Award for his ministry to country music people and fans.

He's also produced a film of the nostalgic last night in the Ryman Auditorium when he preached. He hopes to present it as a Public Broadcasting System special.

Perhaps the altar in Evangel Temple should also be named a historic spot. Since the late sixties, scores of performers and songwriters, including some of the biggest names in the industry, have knelt and left their tears there. Most are still in Nashville, but Jimmie doesn't see much of them anymore.

One of the faithful through the years at Evangel Temple has been Ernest Tubb's daughter, Elaine, also one of the first converts. After joining the church, she was divorced from her songwriter husband, Wayne Walker, who blamed Jimmie and the church for the breakup, vowing that he would rather die than ever set foot in the church.

Before and after his divorce, Wayne Walker

wrote over 7,000 songs, including many top hits, which have sold millions of records. Some were: "Are You Sincere?" (Andy Williams), "How Do You Think I Feel?" (Elvis Presley), "Have You Got Leavin' on Your Mind?" (Patsy Cline), and "I've Got a New Heartache" (Ray Price). Wayne is in the Songwriters' Hall of Fame.

He never submerged his bitter feelings about Jimmie Snow and Evangel Temple. Then in 1979 at fifty-one he contracted cancer. His daughter, Capri, who continued to attend the church with her mother, asked Jimmie to visit him at the hospital. Jimmie went very reluctantly. "I knew he hated me worse than anybody," Jimmie says. "I went mainly because of Capri.

"Wayne was curious about my coming to see him but didn't say much. I could feel the tension, so I had a minute of prayer with him and left.

"He knew he was dying. Two weeks later he called and asked me to come back. I went and sat down by his bed. He leaned over and said, 'Jimmie, you know how much I've hated you.'

"I said, 'Yes, Wayne, I do.'

"He said, 'Do you think you could find it in your heart to forgive me?'

"I said, 'Sure, Wayne. No problem.'

"Then he said, 'Before you leave, would you help me find God? I know I'm going to die. I want to get saved and be ready to meet the Lord.' So I led him to Jesus.

"Before I left, he asked me to pray that God

would help him get out of the hospital. 'I want to come to the church and make my profession public,' he said. 'I want everybody to know.'

"The very next Sunday he was there. Elaine, who had remarried after the divorce, was sitting in the congregation with her husband. When I gave the invitation, Wayne got up and came down the aisle, crying. I got down with him at the altar and we cried and prayed together. Then he stood up and gave this testimony:

"'I know that my time is limited and I don't have long to live. I want you all to know that I'm right with the Lord and with this church. I also want to say that I've written hundreds of songs, had big cars and fortunes, and done everything in the world. But I've never had an experience like this.'

"Wayne asked me to preach his funeral and I said I would. He arranged for his daughter to get up before me and explain to everybody why I was the preacher since Wayne wouldn't have time to get around to tell all his friends and explain what had happened. He died six months later and I preached the funeral. The biggest people in Nashville show business were there. I gave the altar call and fourteen prayed the sinner's prayer with me in the funeral home."

Many of Jimmie's converts seem to slip through the net drawn at Evangel Temple. In a recent service he asked for the hands of those present who had been "saved" in his church since the first of the year. "Eight out of 152," he said sadly. "We've got to have better follow-up."

One reason may be Jimmie's strong preaching. "It's a disgrace to stand at the door of this church and blow smoke in people's faces," he said in that same service. "You may get mad and say, 'I don't like that, Preacher.' Well, that's just tough. Come out from among them and be separate.

"This is a sex-crazed age we're living in. I don't know who's going with who anymore. People change husbands and wives like they change suits and dresses.

"You can stay away from this church, but I'll haunt you to your grave," he said with a wry smile. "When you go to heaven, the first person you see will be me."

Jimmie looked out over his congregation to see the reaction. For a few seconds there was only stark silence; then someone clapped, setting off a burst of applause.

A lot of people around Nashville still love and respect Jimmie Snow.

Meanwhile the Lord's Chapel keeps growing. One of the most recent worshipers is Bobby Wood, who started singing with his family in Baptist churches back in Mississippi and then moved to Memphis where he worked with Elvis Presley, Jerry Lee Lewis, and B. J. Thomas.

"Back then I suspected Elvis was on medication real heavy," Bobby recalls. "B. J. Thomas was in worse shape. He'd taken so many uppers and downers that he got to be like an eighty-year-old man. He got so far out that he would even pull a gun on you and not even realize you were his best friend. I'd always point him to the Lord. He knew that was where I was coming from, even though I wasn't walking with the Lord at that time. Later B. J. got his life straightened out. He's serving the Lord today."

When Bobby moved to Nashville, he got a couple of records out that did well. "If I'm a Fool" was number one in the charts in 1963. He also wrote songs. Crystal Gayle, Loretta Lynn's little sister, had a hit with "You've Been Talkin' in Your Sleep," written by Bobby Wood and Roger Cook.

"I thought I had life made and the world by the tail," Bobby says. "Then the Lord straightened me out."

Bobby left Nashville in a station wagon with five other musicians to perform in Ohio. About 5:00 A.M. the wagon hit a semi head on. The truck driver died in the wreck; the musicians went to the hospital in an ambulance.

"They sewed me up and rolled me out of the operating room 'dead'," Bobby recalls. "They left me in the corridor for an orderly to take me to the morgue. A black doctor happened to come by and saw my arm flop out from under the sheet. Normally he would have just put the arm back, but something told him to feel for a pulse. He felt a faint beat. The doctors went back to work. When I came around, that doctor told me, 'Young man, if you don't believe in God now, there's no hope for you.'"

Afterwards, Bobby met a girl named Janice in a recording studio. They were married and had two sons. Though they started attending church, they couldn't find one they liked.

Bobby says, "I went to see a friend get baptized at the Lord's Chapel. I hadn't felt the Holy Spirit that way since I was a child. At the time, I was struggling to give up drugs. One Tuesday night I went for counseling. They prayed for me to receive the Holy Spirit. I didn't sense any great change until somebody offered me a joint two weeks later. I turned it down just like that. Next it was booze. I turned that down. Then it was a toot of cocaine and I said no without even thinking about it. When I realized what I'd done, I knew it had to be the Lord. I hadn't been able to do that by myself.

"You feel real freedom of worship at the Lord's Chapel. You don't feel condemned if you want to raise your hand and say 'Amen,' 'Praise the Lord,' or whatever. Nobody's gonna be starin' at you if you want to shout 'Hallelujah!' Nobody cares what you wear. It's the Lord's house, open to everybody."

Bobby and Janice are involved in a Friday night Bible study and intercessory prayer group: "We have a long prayer list. I don't know how many people we've marked off as having met the Lord. One who was recently saved in our house is the wife of a top songwriter in town."

Bobby is presently concentrating on songwriting and doing recording sessions. Known as one of the best studio artists in Nashville, he works with George Jones, Tammy Wynette, Loretta Lynn, and other top stars.

"One night I got a chance to witness to Loretta. She wanted to read my palms. I said, 'No, thank you, Loretta. I don't believe in that stuff.'

"She asked, 'Why don't you?'

"'I'm a Christian,' I said.

"'Well, I used to be a member of the Church of Christ. I was raised that way and got baptized,' she replied.

"I said, 'I used to be a Baptist, but now I'm a Christian.' Loretta knows that it isn't a denomination or religion. It's God and you. If she'd turn her life over to the Lord, she'd be a real testimony. I think most people like her want to believe."

Many persons continue to come to the Lord's Chapel in search of a solution to a personal crisis. Vic Willis, baptized a Mormon, later became an Episcopalian. When the chips were down in his life, the tough, white-haired entertainer went to his friends at the Lord's Chapel for help.

Born one of six sons to a fiddling coal miner, Vic grew up in Oklahoma. With two brothers, Guy and Skeeter, Vic formed the Oklahoma Wranglers trio.

World War II interrupted their career and landed Vic on Normandy Beach on D day. He and three buddies were hit by an artillery shell. His friends were killed on the spot, and Vic was seriously wounded with a thigh wound. He prayed, "Lord, if you'll get me out of this, I'll be the best person who ever lived. I'll serve you. I'll do anything you want." However, when the shooting stopped, he returned to his customary cursing and dirty jokes.

After the war the Oklahoma Wranglers became the Willis Brothers. Joining the Grand Ole Opry in 1946, they later left to become the nucleus of Eddie Arnold's network radio and stage show. Then they became the first group to sing backup for the late Hank Williams, as well as the first featured act on the "Jubilee USA" show at Springfield, Missouri. They gave a premiere performance as the first country entertainers to play Washington, D.C.'s Constitution Hall, usually reserved for classical musicians. In 1960 they rejoined the Opry.

Over a span of three decades the Willis Brothers appeared on over 1,500 television shows, sold millions of records, and toured the world. With Guy emceeing on the guitar, Skeeter as the "smilin' fiddler," and baby brother Vic doubling as accordionist and pianist, they became one of the top country and western acts of modern times. Vic also developed a successful jingle business—writing rhymes for radio and television commercials for such corporate clients as Ford, General Motors, and Kellogg's cereals.

Despite his success, however, Vic was no stranger to sorrow. In the mid-fifties he had lost his father to black lung disease and his mother to cancer in 1960. Then in 1974 his brother Harold died. Skeeter, his fellow performer and brother, died in 1976. Shortly afterwards, brothers Joe and Guy were diagnosed as having terminal cancer. His other brother was critically ill with emphysema.

Vic brought on C. W. Mitchell and Curtis Young to keep up the trio. When C. W. was out for a while with a broken back, Vic joked on the Opry, "Just call us the Blue Cross boys."

In July 1978 Vic's fellow entertainers elected him executive director of the Association of Country Entertainers to succeed the late George Morgan. It was around this time that Vic's life began falling apart.

Under the impossible load of being performer, executive director of ACE, husband to his wife, Joyce, and father to his twin daughters, in addition to visiting his hospitalized brothers, Vic developed an ulcer. When it began hemorrhaging, his doctor sent him to the hospital.

Though the rest was helpful, he soon fell into a deep depression. For the first time he began having serious marital problems. "I wasn't getting along with my wife," Vic remembers. "I wasn't thinking clearly. It got so that I didn't like entertainers or hardly anyone. Day after day, I would go into my office, take the phone off the hook, and refuse to answer the door or my mail.

"During this time I became involved with another woman. I finally had to admit this to my wife. She sued for divorce which she should have done. Joe and Guy died, leaving me with only one brother, who was still very sick. I had a complete breakdown and was admitted to a psychiatric ward.

"A Catholic priest and an Episcopal priest tried to help me. The psychiatrist said I had suppressed everything—the grief over my brothers' deaths and the turmoil over my divorce.

"During all this my former wife, my daughters, and my friends at the Opry stood behind me. When I got out of the hospital, my former wife felt we couldn't go back, but she said we could continue to be good friends, and we have.

"Still in a deep depression, I blamed myself for everything. I prayed for forgiveness, but I couldn't forgive myself. The psychiatrist wanted me back in the hospital, but I told him, 'I'm going to fight this out for myself.'

"Still I couldn't snap out of it. I started thinking of ways to commit suicide. A friend asked me if I had nerve enough to go through with it. I said, 'I fought at Normandy. I saw men shot in half. I was wounded and survived. That oughta tell you something.'

"'Maybe I'll ram my car into a bridge abutment,' I told this friend. 'I could jump into the river, take a parachute lesson and forget to pull the cord, or take a '38 and blow my brains out. That'd be real quick.'"

Long suspicious and critical of Opry entertainers who talked about God, the Bible, and salvation, he resented people telling him, "God bless you." He thought they were hypocrites and said so when they were out of earshot.

The board of directors of ACE asked him to continue as executive director. Moved by this show of support, Vic began seeing his colleagues in a different light. One day during a board meeting at which Hank Snow, Barbara Mandrell, Roy Acuff, and Connie Smith were present, he said, "During the past few months, I've learned a lot about you, my fellow entertainers, a lot that I didn't know before. I've grown to love, respect, and appreciate you for your goodness."

He looked directly at Connie Smith. "I'm sorry that I've been sarcastic and critical behind your back, Connie. I've come to believe that you're a good Christian girl. I love all of you." He sat down in tears.

When the depression continued, Vic's former wife asked him to consider spiritual help. When Vic agreed, she suggested calling Connie Smith's pastor. "You've told me a number of times that she's a real Christian. I'll set up an appointment for you," she offered.

That was December 1, 1979. Mrs. Willis made the appointment and Vic, looking ten years older than his fifty-eight years, drove over to the Lord's Chapel.

Finding Connie's preacher, Billy Ray Moore, easy to talk to, Vic says, "I bared my soul to him, told him everything."

"He said, 'Vic, you've got all this guilt. You've asked God to forgive you, and he has. Everybody else has forgiven you, but you.

Now why would you ask God to forgive you, when you won't forgive yourself?'

"It took weeks for that to sink in. I felt like the awfulest person in the whole world. Brother Moore kept assuring me, 'God erased that. It's erased, gone, no more. Accept God's Word that he's forgiven you.'

"I went to the service and saw 1,300 people praising the Lord in song. People would walk up and put their arms around my neck and say, 'I love you.' Some didn't even know who I was.

"I was flooded with love. Overwhelmed. I told my neighbor Clarence, 'You've gotta go over there to the Lord's Chapel with me.'

"He said, 'What do you like about it so much?'

"I said, 'They love you. They really do. They come up and grab you and say, "I love you, brother." If you want to sing, it's OK. If not, don't sing. You hear people that can't sing very good; then you hear somebody like Connie Smith with a beautiful voice come out above everybody. She's sitting there by her fine husband, her lap full of kids. You're listening. She starts clapping her hands, then looks up at you, and smiles. Others are clapping and smiling. It's wonderful.'

"'Clarence,' I kept on, 'you gotta go. You see people with long hair, beards, blacks, whites, young people, all kinds. They're carrying Bibles. They know Christ. They know what love is and they come and hug you, a complete stranger, and say they love you. I tell you, Clarence, you gotta go.'

"He hasn't gone yet," Vic says, "but I expect he will just to shut me up.

"I need all the counseling I can get," Vic admits, yet he also sees the world around him changing for the better. "Being a Christian is a new thing, a wonderful thing. I see more and more people coming to the Lord. People don't down Christians as they used to. Entertainers are not ashamed backstage at the Opry to walk up, hug one another, and say, 'I love you.'

"We always helped one another when we were sick by sending flowers and visiting at the hospital. Now a lot of us send Scripture verses we think are suited to a person's need. Sometimes we get together and pray in a dressing room. It isn't a preachy thing. We're just getting closer to one another and to the Lord."

Vic Willis speaks out of the fresh vitality of a profound spiritual experience. He's heard many hymns sung by entertainers who had a bottle and a woman waiting after the show. He's well aware of the difference between the real and unreal.

Another church which has determined to have a ministry to the country music world is the Two Rivers Baptist Church. Strategically located across Briley Parkway from Opryland, the Opry House, and the Opryland Hotel, it enjoys a close relationship with WSM and the Opry. Pastor Ralph Stone, who grew up listening to country music in central Georgia, opens WSM-TV's broadcast day with a morning devotional. The Sunday morning worship service is also televised over WSM.

Two Rivers has a special early Sunday school class for Opryland performers and holds an Easter sunrise service at Opryland. In return, the Opry allows Two Rivers to use the Opry House for their special Easter services.

Dr. Stone says, "We aren't hung up on rigid structure. We lean more toward a loose worship service, not as far as the Pentecostals, but not nearly as stiff as the formal churches. We're already reaching some country music people. I recently baptized one of the Opry's staff musicians, and we intend to win more to Christ."

In the summer of 1980, Two Rivers featured "Old-fashioned Day." Dr. Stone wore a black string tie, and his family came to church in a buggy. The members dressed in old-fashioned clothes and sang old-time hymns and gospel songs like "I'll Fly Away," taboo in many modern churches. Dr. Stone preached an "old-time sermon" from an 1868 Bible and gave an altar call. Then the people enjoyed dinner on the grounds and a Sunday afternoon "sing." For the occasion, the deacons placed tombstones on the hill behind the church to simulate the customary graveyard, thereby causing visitors to remark that they didn't know Two Rivers had a cemetery. "Our folks ate it up,"

Dr. Stone says. "We didn't leave until 4:00 P.M."

Most of all, Dr. Stone wants "a Spirit-filled church where the Spirit moves mightily. Then you'll have a super-charged emotional experience from the Lord because God works through our emotions. He's not restricted from allowing us to weep, shout 'Amen,' and applaud."

Still, Dr. Stone sees high emotionalism as a problem in church. He asks, "Does the emotionalism become an end in itself? Are we there just to get an emotional high? I think as you experience a closeness to Christ, you'll have a surge of emotion. But it should be transferred into Christian commitment all week long."

In 1980 the Music City Christian Fellowship was formed to help Christians in the Nashville music world accomplish this goal. Not a church, the Fellowship is organized along the same lines as the Christian Medical Society and the Christian Businessmen's Committee.

Joe Babcock was elected the first president; Billy Walker, vice president; and Emily Bradshaw Weiland, secretary-treasurer. The Reverends Billy Ray Moore and Joe Dee Kelly, executive director for the Assemblies of God in Tennessee, served as ministerial counselors.

The founders stated as the purpose of the Fellowship:

> To win souls to Christ through action and prayer; to encourage bold witnessing within the music and entertainment indus-

try as well as reaching out to others; to nurture strength among us by the assembling of the body in unity and love; to provide fellowship for believers within the industry that we might be brought closer together; to encourage the teaching and the studying of the Word of God according to the commission given us by our Lord Jesus Christ; to provide a sponsoring organization to carry out various worthwhile projects, such as evangelistic services, television programs, counseling services, a Music Row chapel, and any other works and ministries that God would lead us to do; to encourage righteous living and faithful stewardship among ourselves and those around us; to influence for the good the music and entertainment industry.

For the first few weeks the group met for prayer and sharing in the conference room of Broadcast Music, Incorporated, a block down from the Country Music Hall of Fame. They now get together every Thursday noon in the Maranatha Christian Bookstore across from the Belmont Church of Christ on Music Row.

At a recent meeting of the Fellowship, Marijohn Wilkin reported on a Christian novel she had just read called *In His Steps Today*. The songwriter challenged her fellow believers to "try to do everything for one week the way you think Jesus would."

Delores Edgin, who sings with the "Nashville Additions" on "Hee-Haw," shared a witnessing experience she had had on the set.

Bill Walker (no relation to Opry singer, Billy Walker), a music director and arranger of many country music specials on network television, told of a recent recording session with Johnny Cash. "Johnny called me out of the group. I thought, *Boy, what have I done now*? All he said was, 'Let's have a little prayer together.' That made my day!"

Joe Babcock described a recording session in which he balked at singing an offensive word. "It messed up the record and the director flared up at me. I offered to pay for the damage, but he cooled off. However, I haven't gotten any work from him since. I'm trying to spread the word around that we don't do that kind of material."

"Before my last recording session," recalled Delores Edgin, "we Christians prayed. By the way, what do you do when they come up and tell a dirty joke and you don't know it when they start?"

"I can tell you what happened at a session last night," said Bobby Wood. "The jokes kept getting raunchier and raunchier. Three of us there were Christians. We didn't laugh. After a while they got the message."

"Well, the percentage of Christians in music has been going up," observed Bill Walker. "We're not perfect. We're human. We're only forgiven." The meeting continued with more sharing and ended with prayer.

Right from the start of the organization, Fellowship members prayed for an opportunity

to present a joint Christian witness. One afternoon Sandy Posey Robinson, who attends the
Lord's Chapel and had some big hits in the
sixties, called Joe and Carol Babcock to dis-
cuss the idea of presenting an evangelistic
service. It would be held at the close of the
annual spring Fan Fair attended by thousands
of country music lovers. With the Babcocks'
encouragement, Sandy began calling other
members.

The result was "Sunday Morning Country,"
a service to be presented in the War Memorial
Auditorium at the close of Fan Fair. It would
not compete with local churches since the service was on behalf of out-of-town visitors.

Despite very little promotion, about 600 fans
showed up. Before going onstage, Billy Walker,
the country singer, led Fellowship members
in prayer, claiming "the authority of Jesus
and the Holy Spirit over every demonic force
in this building."

LuLu Roman sang and gave her testimony.
Billy Walker was to be on next. When emcee,
Biff Collie, introduced Billy, a man from the
audience ran up, grabbed the microphone,
and began singing a frenzied version of "How
Great Thou Art." Biff and Billy tried to get
him off, but he refused to budge. Then Billy
simply walked over to him, touched him on
the forehead, and prayerfully said one word,
"Jesus!" The man became so disoriented that
he had to be helped offstage.

After finishing his song and testimony, Billy
walked outside to see what had happened to

the man. He spotted him sitting bent over on a railing. When Billy started talking to him, he went into a frenzy again. Billy put his hand on the man's head and prayed. As Billy turned around, the man went over the railing. "It looked like a force threw him over," Billy says. The man hit the ground several feet below and lay still. Billy quickly called an ambulance to take him to the hospital.

That night Billy talked to the man's wife, who reported he had a broken back and a skull injury. Billy called several people in the Fellowship to pray for the injured man. The next night Billy checked with his wife, who told him that X-rays now showed his back was fine and that he would be discharged from the hospital in a few days. The couple went home to New Jersey the following weekend. Billy and Betty Walker put a minister in New Jersey in touch with them and they accepted Christ.

A dozen others made professions of faith at the close of the "Sunday Morning Country" in the auditorium. The Fellowship decided to repeat the service at the close of the annual deejay convention in October.

This time more Christian artists, including Connie Smith and George Hamilton IV, participated. Again no effort was made to invite local church people.

Various artists gave their testimonies.

Billy Walker was the first to share with the audience: "We're still in the country music business and still singing our country songs, and one thing we share in common is Jesus Christ. A few years ago I had a number one hit song and I was, of all people, most miserable. I had everything you could speak of and yet, in my heart, I had nothing. I said, 'What is this? Why can't I be happy? Why can't I be the kind of person I want to be?' Something spoke to me and said, *You don't have what it takes to be anything*.

"I said, 'Lord, if fame and money cannot satisfy, I want whatever will.' When I gave Christ my life, that longing was met.

"Everything doesn't always go as I want it to, but praise God, I've got Somebody that sticks with me through thick and thin. Hallelujah! His name is Jesus, and I recommend him to you."

Connie Smith followed Billy with her word of testimony: "My life began when I chose Jesus and became God's child. He grows sweeter and sweeter. I gave up my music. It had become a curse in my life, but when I gave my heart to Jesus, he gave my music right back to me."

Teddy Wilburn came on and said, "I was drunk for five-and-a-half years and maybe sober thirty evenings out of that whole time. I thought life had done me in. People had done me in. I couldn't cope and instead of going to Jesus, I went to the bottle. I found no answer there and my life only continued to get worse.

"I praise God that he touched my life in February 1976. I now have a personal relationship with Jesus Christ. I appreciate this. I don't understand it. I don't know why he loves me. But I sure do love him.

"I don't know how many of you have really reached bottom in your lives. But I know what it is to be without a friend. I've been there. I found that Jesus could take the mess of my life and make something beautiful. I found that he could be the perfect Friend, one who nevers lets me down."

Marijohn Wilkin testified next: "After all these wonderful testimonies, what more can I say? I was like Teddy and Billy and Connie. I also know what it's like to feel that there's no one to turn to. I know what it means to find Jesus as the Savior who can heal and forgive. After I accepted him and gave him my life, I wondered how I could make it. He told me, 'Just follow me one step at a time.'" She then sang "One Step at a Time" and got a standing ovation.

After other songs and testimonies, Joe Dee Kelley, founder of the Assembly of God church in Brentwood, gave a short message and invited people to accept Christ. They came from every section of the auditorium seeking the Lord.

Believing that their ministry is just beginning, the Music City Christian Fellowship would like to go on evangelistic tour, do a network special, and hold a crusade in Nashville or some other town. They are willing to give their services free as an offering to the Lord.

Joe Dee Kelley believes a religious revival

has begun in the Nashville music community: "We are seeing people saved and Christians come forth to witness in proportions unthought of ten years ago. I can't tell you what particular church they all attend. We are all active in some congregation, but we don't think of ourselves as Baptist, Assembly of God, or Methodist. We're Christians first of all."

Joe Babcock nods his head. "This isn't something that the promoters thought up. This is an act of the Holy Spirit."